Vietnam and Cambodia t

The Vietnam and Travel Guide 2023-2024

Experience the Unique Cultures and Traditions with your Family

Ortega W. Susan

Vietnam and Cambodia travel guide 2023-2024

All rights reserved. No part of this publication may be reproduced, distributed, or transmitted in any form or by any means, including photocopying, recording, or other electronic or mechanical methods, without the prior written permission of the publisher, except in the case of brief quotations embodied in critical reviews and certain other noncommercial uses permitted by copyright law.

Copyright © Ortega W. Susan,2023

Vietnam and Cambodia travel guide 2023-2024

Disclaimer

The information in this travel guide book is based on the author's personal experiences and research, and is accurate to the best of the author's knowledge at the time of publication. However, things change quickly, and the author cannot guarantee that all of the information in this book will be completely accurate or up-to-date at the time of your travels.

Please use your own judgment and discretion when planning and making decisions about your trip. The author and publisher of this book are not responsible for any losses, damages, or injuries that may occur as a result of using the information in this book.

In addition, the author and publisher of this book do not endorse or recommend any of the businesses or services listed in this book. Any links to third-party websites are provided for your convenience only, and the author and publisher are not responsible for the content or accuracy of any third-party websites.

Please travel safely and responsibly

About the Author

Ortega W. Susan is a passionate and adventurous writer with a deep love for exploring the world and sharing her experiences through captivating travel guides. Born with a wanderlust spirit and an insatiable curiosity, Ortega has dedicated her life to uncovering the hidden gems of our planet and crafting informative and inspiring travel narratives for fellow adventurers. Ortega brings a unique perspective to the world of travel writing. Her writing style combines vivid descriptions, practical advice, and a genuine appreciation for the cultures and landscapes she encounters. Each of her travel guides is a meticulously researched and thoughtfully curated resource designed to help readers embark on unforgettable journeys. Ortega's journey as a travel writer began with a solo backpacking trip through Southeast Asia, where she discovered her talent for blending storytelling with practical travel information. Since then, she has explored countless destinations across the globe, in addition to her travel writing, Ortega is an advocate for sustainable tourism and responsible travel practices. She believes that travelers have a responsibility to protect and preserve the places they visit, and her guides often include tips on eco-friendly travel and cultural sensitivity. When she's not on the road or writing about her travels, Ortega enjoys photography, hiking, and trying new cuisines from around the world. She resides in a cozy cottage in the countryside, where she finds solace and inspiration for her next writing adventure.

Join Ortega on her journey of exploration, discovery, and storytelling as she continues to inspire and empower travelers to embark on unforgettable adventures. Explore the world through her eyes, and let her travel guides be your compass on your next adventure.

Vietnam and Cambodia travel guide 2023-2024

TABLE OF CONTENTS

INTRODUCTION 9
- ❖ Visiting Vietnam and Cambodia in five days 11
- ❖ Organizing Your Adventure as a Family 15
- ❖ What to anticipate from this travel manual 17

DESTINATIONS IN VIETNAM 19

BUDGET FOR CAMBODIA 41
- ❖ Places to Go in Cambodia 43

CULTURE AND TRADITIONS 59
- ❖ Vietnamese Heritage & Culture 59
- ❖ Vietnam's Dos and Don'ts of Etiquette 67

CAMBODIAN CULTURE AND TRADITIONS 72
- ❖ Customary gender roles for men and women ... 75
- ❖ Traditional ideas and religion 77
- ❖ Cambodian Manners and Etiquette 83

GASTRONOMIC PLEASURE 95
- ❖ Cambodian cuisine you must taste 101
- ❖ Cambodia's top restaurants to visit 103

VISA AND ENTRY REQUIREMENTS AND
ACCOMMODATION OPTIONS 109
- ❖ Cambodian Accommodation Options. 113
- ❖ Vietnam Accommodation Options................... 119

- ❖ Tips for Health and Safety 130
- SHOPPING IN VIETNAM AND CAMBODIA 133
- CONCLUSION 139
  - ❖ Packing Necessities 139

Vietnam and Cambodia travel guide 2023-2024

Vietnam and Cambodia travel guide 2023-2024

INTRODUCTION

Once upon a time, in the heart of Southeast Asia, there lay two magical lands: Vietnam and Cambodia. These two countries, rich in culture and history, have captivated travelers from all over the world for centuries.

Vietnam, a land of lush green landscapes, ancient temples, and vibrant cities, is a feast for the senses. From the bustling streets of Hanoi to the serene waters of Ha Long Bay, Vietnam offers something for everyone.

Cambodia, on the other hand, is a land of ancient mysteries and hidden wonders. From the awe-inspiring temples of Angkor Wat to the charming villages along the Mekong River, Cambodia is a place where time seems to stand still.

But what makes Vietnam and Cambodia truly special is their people. Warm and welcoming, the Vietnamese and Cambodian people are always eager to share their culture and traditions with visitors.

So if you're looking for a family vacation that is both educational and unforgettable, look no further than Vietnam and Cambodia. Together, these two countries offer a unique and enriching experience that will stay with you for a lifetime.

Imagine your family exploring the ancient temples of Angkor Wat, learning about the Khmer Empire, and taking a boat cruise down the Mekong River. Imagine your children tasting delicious Vietnamese and Cambodian cuisine, and making friends with the locals.

A Vietnam and Cambodia family vacation are a journey that will create lasting memories for the whole family. So, pack your bags, get ready for an adventure, and discover the magic of Vietnam and Cambodia!

LET'S GO!!!

Vietnam and Cambodia travel guide 2023-2024

❖ Visiting Vietnam and Cambodia in five days

Day 1

Your first day's activities in Vietnam, Cambodia- Transportation from the airport to the hotel in the Old Quarter of Hanoi; - Water puppet shows, My Village Show, and An O Show available; - Incredible Hanoi street food tour
Details…………..

Day 2

Hanoi, the Halong Bay "paradise on Earth"
What to do on your second day in Cambodia Thailand Beautiful journey from Hanoi to Halong sea - Budget-friendly to luxurious Halong cruises ranging from 3 to 5 stars - Sailing among 1969 limestone islands in the sea - Swimming in the water - Kayaking and cave discovery - Onboard spa
Details………….

Vietnam and Cambodia travel guide 2023-2024

Day 3

Ninhbinh province's Tamcoc and Halong Bay

Your third day's activities in Vietnam, Cambodia sailing around Halong Bay, seeing caves, going kayaking, and taking a 3.5-hour trip to Ninhbinh Province. In Ninhbinh for the night

Day 4

Grand Circuit – Angkor Wat – Siem Reap
Grand Circuit - Angkor Thom - Angkor Wat
You will go to Angkor Wat, a World Heritage Site, in the morning. Let's begin with the South Gate of Angkor Thom, which is well-known for its numerous enormous stone portraits of people. The Phimeanakas, the Royal Enclosure, the Elephant Terrace, the magnificent Bayon Temple, and the Terrace of the Leper King are the next stops on your tour of Cambodia. The architectural wonder that is Angkor Wat will always be a part of your journey.

We meander about this enormous monument, taking in the numerous halls with columns, libraries, pavilions, courtyards, and water-filled ponds that mirror the soaring temple.

Lunch at a nearby eatery. Next, go to the Preah Khan temple, which was constructed by Preah Khan, King Jayavarman VII. Similar to Ta Prohm, this temple has passages that embrace the shoulders and towering enclosures. It is in a respectable condition of preservation with continuous restoration work, unlike Ta Prohm. You continue your journey to NeakPean, a fountain that symbolizes the idyllic Himalayan mountain lake and is built in the middle of a pool; Ta Som, Eastern Mebon; and Pre Rup, the mountain temple that is open until dusk and defended by stone statues of harnessed elephants, some of which are still in a respectable state of preservation. Spend the night in the hotel.

Day 5: Departure from Cambodia

See the temples at Bakong, PrahKo, and Lolei; do a short circle; stay within Chef D'Angkor; depart from Siem Reap. Finish your amazing tour in Vietnam and Cambodia.

Explore the Roluos group in the morning; it is located 15 km (10 miles) southwest of Siem Reap. Three temples: Bakong, PrahKo, and Lolei are part of the group. The temples, which bear the name Lolei, were constructed in the late ninth century and correlate to the former capital of Hariharalaya. Three old Hindu temples that have been conserved to a remarkable degree will astound you. Some of the oldest surviving examples of Khmer art are the bas-reliefs. Villages of today around the temples.

Lunch at a nearby eatery. Your Vietnam Cambodia trip continues in the afternoon with a fascinating visit to the tiny circuit with Prasat Kravan's distinctive brick sculptures, the Ta Prohm entwined with the forest. This location served as the set for the well-known Angelina Jolie film Tomb Raider. Ta Prohm, a well-known shrine in the region Enjoy a leisurely tour around this amazing location, where enormous fig and kapok trees choke the historic masonry in a striking display of the interaction between man and nature. Proceed to Takeo, Thommanon, and Chau Say Tevoda on your journey. Chef D'Angkor's dinner and Spend the night at the hotel.

Continue for details ……………

Vietnam and Cambodia travel guide 2023-2024

❖ Organizing Your Adventure as a Family

Arranging a trip to Vietnam and Cambodia with your family doesn't have to be difficult. A little preparation will go a long way toward making the trip fun and instructive for all participants.

- ✓ **Select the appropriate locations.** Given the size and diversity of Vietnam and Cambodia, it's essential to select travel locations that suit the requirements and interests of your family. For instance, you might choose Vietnam concentrate on family-friendly locations like Hanoi, Hoi An, and Siem Reap if you have little children.
- ✓ **Make a thorough itinerary.** It's time to start organizing your itinerary when you've decided on your destinations. Make sure to account for the time needed for rest and relaxation in addition to the travel time between locations. Including some wiggle room in your schedule is also a smart idea in case anything unforeseen comes up.

- ✓ **Make reservations for your travel and lodging in advance.** This is particularly crucial if you're going during the busiest time of year. Both Vietnam and Cambodia provide a wide range of family-friendly lodging choices, so you're likely to find something that fits your needs and budget.
- ✓ **Obtain traveler's insurance.** Any family vacation needs travel insurance, but trips to Vietnam and Cambodia require it even more. It's crucial to obtain travel insurance in case of any medical crises because these nations' healthcare systems differ from those of many Western nations.
- ✓ **Be prepared for any kind of weather.** Due to their tropical climates, Vietnam and Cambodia should be prepared for hot, muggy weather. But it's also crucial to prepare for chilly weather, particularly if you're going to the highlands or going somewhere in the winter.

Vietnam and Cambodia travel guide 2023-2024

❖ What to anticipate from this travel manual

All the information you want to organize a family trip to Vietnam and Cambodia in 2023–2024 may be found in this travel guide. Everything from picking the best travel places to preparing for your vacation to maintaining your health and safety will be covered.

Here's a more thorough rundown of what to anticipate from this travel guide:

An overview of Cambodia and Vietnam You'll get a quick rundown of the two nations' histories, cultures, and geographical features in this section.

Organizing your travel: Everything from picking the best places to making travel and lodging arrangements to packing for your vacation will be covered in this section.

Actions to take: You may find a list of family-friendly sites and activities in Vietnam and Cambodia in this area.

Advice for taking kids on vacation: You may find advice on how to travel safely and healthily with kids in Vietnam and Cambodia in this area, along with suggestions on where to go and what to bring.

The conclusion, this part offers some last advice on how to maximize your family trip in Vietnam and Cambodia.

Vietnam and Cambodia travel guide 2023-2024

DESTINATIONS IN VIETNAM

Vietnam is one of Southeast Asia's top family vacation spots because of its stunning natural surroundings, historical landmarks, warm welcome, and eye-catching attractions.

This nation is full of incredible discoveries to be made, from the traditional beauty of old buildings and historical legacies to the natural attractiveness of breathtaking beaches and landscapes. Vietnam has a wide range of enjoyable and thrilling activities that may really satisfy everyone's interests.

There are plenty of kid-friendly attractions in the nation, such as aquarium displays, amusement water parks, and more, making it a popular location for family vacations. You won't have to worry about finding anything to do or where to go with your adorable children. Everybody can always find something to do here. To choose the ideal attraction for your family's holiday, let's look through a list of them.

➢ **Ha Noi**

This city offers a wealth of national culture, mouthwatering local cuisine, and a plethora of other wonderful family-friendly activities. Walking through the Old Quarter's tiny streets and stopping at street sellers is a terrific way to begin exploring. Your family will be able to see a variety of unusual traditional objects in addition to real Vietnamese food.

In addition, Hanoi has a number of museums where you and your children may learn about Vietnam's history and cultural richness. The Vietnam Museum of Ethnology, for instance, provides visitors with a wealth of information on Vietnamese ethnicities, as do other museums with distinctive features like the Ho Chi Minh Museum and the Hoa Lo Prison Museum.

The Thang Long Water Puppet Theatre is one of the most amazing places to see in Hanoi. Your family is welcome to witness the age-old art form of water puppetry, in which gracefully moving wooden puppets narrate historical tales about Vietnam to the audience.

Families with energetic kids need to engage in outdoor activities. Heading to the West Lake Water Park will allow you to enjoy incredible games under the blue pool. Alternatively, the greatest option for the whole family is to find a green area to spend time in. Lenin Park and Thu Le Zoo are two examples of green parks that are inside the city limits and offer a clean environment.

Additionally, travelers rank the following meals as must-try Hanoi fare that you should not miss: pho, bun dau mam tom, and bun cha.
However, water puppetry is a kind of old-time entertainment that is excellent for families. The puppeteers will undoubtedly give you a fresh viewpoint.

Recommended Resort & Hotel:
APARTMENT IREST
Location: Trung Liet, Dong Da, Hanoi; 202 Nguyen Van Tuyet
Cost: 50,000 VND to $700,000 per day

The Esplendor Hotel and Spa in Hanoi
Location: Hang Bo, Hoan Kiem, Hanoi; 80 Hang Ga Ward
Cost per day: 1.500.000VND – 2.000.000VND

> ➢ **Bay of Halong**

You won't regret choosing to travel to this location, which offers a few breathtaking scenes. Halong Bay, which is around 165 kilometers from Hanoi's capital, is home to hundreds of untamed limestone islands that rise out of the emerald sea. For a family trip, a cruise is strongly recommended. It's the ideal opportunity to appreciate the island's unspoiled beauty and take part in exciting on-board activities like nighttime squid fishing or Vietnamese cookery classes, which are sure to delight guests of all ages.
On an isolated island, parents and kids alike will enjoy swimming, snorkeling, kayaking, and many other water-based activities. Specifically, your family may go to Cat Ba island and enjoy the white sand beaches there for tanning. For supper, a self-seafood

barbecue is a great suggestion for your family's vacation.

It should come as no surprise that there are a ton of eateries in this area that serve a substantial quantity of seafood at reasonable prices for families with foodies, since there is an abundance of fresh seafood to be found there, including lobster, crab, oysters, and others. The best time to visit this bay is between October and December because to the pleasant weather, which averages 23°C. If you're a young family with small children, pick the appropriate moment to protect their health.

It is certain that your family will never forget their visit to Ha Long Bay. As you approach this country, the azure lake will be dotted with hundreds of limestone mountains. For your family vacation, a boat is strongly suggested as the best way to see the island's unadulterated beauty. To explore the interior of the limestone cave, you and your family will be floating on the water.

If not, you may engage in other amazing boat activities that are available to individuals of all ages, such as night squid fishing or Vietnamese culinary workshops. Swimming, kayaking, and sunset gazing are some other activities.

Recommended Resort & Hotel:
Vietnam Cruise
Location: Tuan Chau, Ha Long City; Tuan Chau 22 Tuan Chau International Port
Cost: Between 11,000 and 15,000 VND each day

➢ Danang

Recognized as the most valuable city in Vietnam to live in, Danang has grown to be a popular family vacation spot. Situated in the heart of Vietnam, it can be effortlessly reached with a one-hour flight from either Hanoi or Ho Chi Minh City. This seaside city is undoubtedly brimming with family-friendly activities and enjoyable places to visit.

You may go outside with your kids to enjoy swimming, surfing, and tanning on some of the most gorgeous beaches in the area, such as My Khe beach and Non Nuoc beach.

Located 40 kilometers east of Danang, Ba Na Hill is one of the most upscale destinations where your family may enjoy the most thrilling amusement options and marvel at the breathtaking French architecture. The finest memories include, in all honesty, getting lost in the French Village, strolling on the fabled Golden Bridge, and riding the cable car to enjoy a panoramic view. If your children enjoy being active, be sure to visit Fantasy Park, where there are tons of exciting games for the whole family to enjoy. With so much waiting to be discovered, Asia Park is a great place to take your kids. Visitors may take in the stunning Asian food from Vietnam, Japan, South Korea, Thailand, India, and other countries, as well as ancient architecture, at the Cultural Park.

Da Nang is located in the middle of Vietnam. One of the greatest spots to travel to Vietnam with family is this site. Families may visit the renowned golden bridge and amusement parks in the Ba Na hill complex.
The Marble Mountains, Lady Buddha, Dragon Bridge, Ba Na Hills, Non Nuoc Beach, Son Tra Mountain, and My Khe Beach are among the locations where you may go sightseeing.
Comfy spa services that are appropriate for all ages are included in the vacation package.

Hotel & Resort Suggested:
Hotel Sala Danang Beach
Address: 36–38 E. Lam Hoanh, Son Tra, Phuoc My, and Da NangCost: 1.500.000VND – 950.000VND per day

➢ **Hoa An**

If you're looking for a less crowded, calmer place to spend time with your loved ones, Hoi An is a great option. This quaint old village is accessible to travelers after a 45-minute trip from Danang. On foot or by bicycle, you may easily tour various scenic spots, temples, and exquisitely preserved homes. Alternatively, a fantastic approach to learn about the local way of life for fisherman is to take a longboat ride down the Thu Bon river.

Visit historical locations such as the Japanese Bridge, Tan Ki House, Fujian Assembly Hall, Chuc Thanh Pagoda, and Hoi An Museum of History & Culture to learn about the lives of the past for yourself and your children.

Magnificent beaches may be found within a few kilometers from the center of this UNESCO-listed ancient town. While visiting Hoi An, take advantage of the cycling and hiking tours available, and explore the surrounding region, which includes hills, rice farms, and immaculate beaches. Gleaming lights and vibrant lanterns will draw your attention right away at night. The 14th and 15th days of the eighth lunar month, which falls in September most of the time, are when the Lantern Festival is held, if you're lucky.

Additionally, the food is very varied; some must-try items are banh bao vac, my Quang, cao lau, and many other delectable meals that cost no more than $2 to $3.

Hoi An is a great option if you wish to spend time with your loved ones in a less hectic and noisy environment. Explore exquisitely renovated residences, temples, and a number of tourist destinations on foot or by bicycle, including the Japanese Bridge, Tan Ki House, Fujian Assembly Hall, Chuc Thanh Pagoda, Hoi An Museum of History & Culture, and An Bang Beach.

Alternatively, taking a longboat ride down the Thu Bon river is a fantastic opportunity to discover more about the life of the local fisherman.

At night, lanterns with brilliant colors and sparkling lights will catch your eye. If you're lucky, you may arrive in time for the Lantern Festival, which takes place on the 14th and 15th day of the eighth lunar month, which often falls in September.

Hotel & Resort Suggested:
La Siesta Resort & Spa in Hoi An
Where: Hoi An, Quang Nam; 132 Hung Vuong, Cam Pho Ward
Cost: 1,700,000VND to 3,000,000VND per day

➢ **Van Quoc**

Families love this island because of its laid-back vibe and plenty of kid-friendly activities. In particular, visitors from all over the world are granted a Phu Quoc visa waiver, which permits them to enter the island nation for stays shorter than 30 days without a visa.

There are several opulent resorts here that your family may choose from for the ideal getaway. Younger children can participate in the recreational activities on the white sand beaches at Long Beach or

Ong Lang beach while their parents enjoy tanning under a beautifully bright day.

Vinpearl Land amusement park is a family-friendly destination that gives youngsters the chance to experience a selection of exhilarating activities and adventures, including rollercoasters, thrilling water slides, 5D cinemas, and a choice of food options. With its diverse collection of animals, Vietnam's largest zoo in particular is sure to thrill children. The lively street performances, daily magic and musical displays, and traditional dances will undoubtedly captivate your children, making it the ideal getaway for families seeking an exciting day on Phu Quoc Island.

Your kids will enjoy exploring the uncommon plants and animals of Phu Quoc National Park, including the long-tailed macaque, silver langurs, sus scofa, and flying fox. A memorable holiday experience that your family should have is a visit to Phu Quoc Prison, where your children may learn about Vietnamese history and understand the value of international peace. It is ideal to visit this island in the dry season, which runs from November to March, when there are bright sky and comfortable temperatures of about 26°C.

Inexpensive: Sea Star Resort, L'Azure Resort and Spa, Cassia Cottage, Peppercorn Beach Resort, Thanh Kieu Beach Resort, Mango Bay Resort, Bauhinia Resort Phu Quoc, and Cottage Village.

Four-star hotels and up: Herbs Spa & Hotel Grand World Phu Quoc ($17 per night), Marina Seaside Boutique Hotel Phu Quoc ($6 per night), Crowne Plaza Phu Quoc Starbay, An IHG Hotel ($95 per night), Regent Phu Quoc ($361 per night).

Two-star accommodations include the Riverside Mini Hotel Grand World Phu Quoc ($25 per night), the Dương Đông Hotel ($13 per night), the Halona Hotel ($8 per night), and the Plus Hotel Phu Quoc ($9 per night).

> **Trung Nha**

This southern Vietnamese coastal vacation city is well-known for its unspoiled islands and sandy beaches. This is the perfect location for your family's island getaway. A thousand coconut palms envelop the resort, creating a tranquil environment and breathtaking view.

For the outdoorsy family, there are also riding, swimming, fishing, and kayaking on sun-kissed beaches. A great way for the whole family to enjoy the expansive view is to take a boat ride throughout their holiday.

Children are captivated by Vin Pearl Amusement Park's water slides, games, huge aquarium, pool, and assortment of rides, while adults appear to be interested in exploring unusual and historic buildings like Po Nagar Cham Towers and Long Son Pagoda. Take your kids to the National Oceanographic Museum of Vietnam, where they may see a variety of vibrant fish as well as some uncommon native aquatic animals including sea horses, sharks, and turtles. In addition to housing hundreds of monkeys, Monkey Island (20 km off the coast of Nha Trang) offers a variety of activities, including a go-kart track and other performance venues.

Try a mud bath; the rich mineral content in the mud is supposed to have therapeutic effects; most people apply the mud to their skin, then lie down in the water to let it do its job.

Families who love the outdoors may also go fishing, kayaking, swimming, or bicycling. A boat cruise is a fantastic way for the whole family to enjoy the wide-ranging views while on vacation.

Adolescents are captivated by VinPearl Amusement Park's water slides, games, huge aquarium, swimming area, and other attractions, while adults are intrigued by the odd and ancient buildings like Po Nagar Cham Towers and Long Son Pagoda.

Recommended Resort & Hotel:
The Anadam
Address: Nguyen Tat Thanh Lot 3, Cam Hai Dong, Cam Lam, Khanh Hoa
Cost per day: 3.500.000VND – 6.200.00VND

> ➤ **Tau Vung**

There's a good reason why Vung Tau is so well-liked by families of all stripes: the white sand beaches, the pristine blue waves, and the abundance of family-friendly activities. You may have thrilling bonding moments with your kids by taking them on powerboat rides or kitesurfing lessons at the sandy beaches such as Bai Sau (Back beach), Bai Dua (Pineapple beach), and Paradise beach.

Savoring the mouthwatering seafood of the town is one of the most important aspects of a family trip. The menus of the majority of the restaurants there feature a variety of freshly prepared, delectable foods including boiling crab, grilled octopus, Vietnamese tiny pancakes (Banh khot), and more.

Explore the oldest lighthouse in Nui Nho Mountain and a massive 105-foot-tall statue of Jesus Christ with your family for a whole day. There are many of family-friendly activities available at Ho May Culture & Ecotourism Park, including paintball, archery, bumper cars, rollercoasters, and go karts in addition to limitless park rides. That's a pretty great place for your kids to go.

There won't be as much sparkle in the sand and beach as there is in Da Nang or Phu Quoc. For the following reasons, nonetheless, this location remains among the greatest family vacation spots in Vietnam: mouthwatering seafood,
If your kids are ready for some daring family fun, you may try kitesurfing or take powerboat rides at the sandy beaches including Bai Sau (Back beach), Bai Dua (Pineapple beach), and Paradise beach.
The 105-foot-tall statue of Jesus Christ and the historic lighthouse atop Nui Nho Mountain are open for your family to explore for the entire day. Family-friendly attractions at Ho May Culture & Ecotourism Park include a cable car ride, unrestricted playground

rides, bumper cars, roller coasters, go-karts, water slides, paintball, and archery. That sounds like a really great place for your kids to vacation.

Recommended Resort & Hotel:

The Hotel Imperial

Address: 159 Thuy Van, Thang Tam Ward, Ba Ria - Vung Tau City, Vung Tau City.

Cost: between 2,000.000VND and 2,0000VNS per day

➢ **Dalat.**

Dalat, often known as the "City of Eternal Spring," has a year-round pleasant environment and an abundance of lovely flowers. There is a plethora of family-friendly activities available, ranging from exploring vast woods to taking in the sights of waterfalls including Elephant Falls, Datanla waterfalls, and Pongour Falls. Love Valley, with its verdant hills and exquisite gardens, is a great place for running, cycling, and paddle boating, especially for both adults and kids. you may visit the Bao Dai Palace Museum, which provides an insight into the life of Vietnam's last emperor, to learn more about the local way of life. There are a few beautiful temples that your family might visit, such as Linh Quang Pagoda and Truc Lam Pagoda. Your children may be enthralled with the magnificent, vibrant statues there.

Lang Biang is the ideal destination for family-friendly activities like farming and hiking to enjoy the area's unparalleled views. Try canyoning if you're an adventurous family; it's a lot of fun.

For children who enjoy sports and games with an element of adventure, the Datanla High Rope course, which is situated in Central Highlands (5km from the center), is the perfect place. A popular activity there is the zip line; feel free to try it without fear because the personnel will walk you through every step with professionalism and ability. Little ones who adore animals will find Zoodoo to be a kid-friendly zoo with a distinct aesthetic. How wonderfully you can feed the squirrels and various birds, or hold the sheep in your hands. Due to the challenging road route and the location in a highland area, families with little children are not advised to visit this location.

➤ **City of Ho Chi Minh**

This city has a long number of family-friendly activities to choose from, including breathtaking locations, a rich cultural heritage, and delicious cuisine. Everything you need to keep your family occupied on vacation is here.

Younger ones will enjoy love the many water parks and amusement parks available, like Dam Sen Water Park, Suoi Tien theme park, Kidcity, Thao Cam Vien, and others.

If you are interested in learning more about Vietnamese history, consider taking the Cu Chi underground trip. The Central Post Office, Notre Dame Cathedral, and the War Remnant Museum are further locations that are well visiting.

However, this city is home to a large number of skyscrapers that combine entertainment with contemporary amenities. The highest structure in Southern Asia, Land Mark 81, offers the finest skyline vista, which you do not want to miss. This is a great place to shop since you can get stylish products for your family as well as a variety of international cuisines to sample.

In this big city, you can easily get thousands of classic foods for $2 to $3 on the street. A day spent taking a cooking lesson and touring the Ben Thanh market is also a terrific choice for your family holiday; your children will be able to learn more about Vietnamese culture and people.

Ho Chi Minh metropolis is the biggest metropolis in Vietnam and among the most kid-friendly places to visit. Any family holiday should include at least three or four days in this old French colonial capital, which is home to Vietnam's tallest skyscrapers and top-notch museums. The Central Post Office, the War Remnants Museum, the Ben Thanh market, and the Notre Dame Cathedral neighborhood are all accessible as tourist destinations in Saigon. The family and you become deeply in love with the food of south Vietnam, particularly with delicacies like Com Tam, Banh Xeo, and Pho. You should also sample some Banh Trang Tron and Hot Vit Lon, two Vietnamese street foods.

Recommended Resort & Hotel:
Harmony Hotel & Spa in Saigon
Address: 34 Bui Thi Xuan, District 1, Pham Ngu Lao Ward, Ho Chi Minh City
Cost per day: 1.400.000VND – 2.000.000VND

➢ Ten. Delta Mekong

If your family is willing to escape the hustle and bustle of the city, the Mekong Delta offers a really serene escape with its extensive network of waterways, wetlands, islands, and rice fields. Its distinct ecology makes it the perfect place for youngsters to discover nature.

The majority of the fruit consumed nationwide comes from the Mekong Delta. For people of all ages, taking a tour of the premises is the most engaging pastime. In the biggest fruit orchards, such as Cai Be and Vinh Long, you may do this to directly take ripe fruit from the trees and consume it right away. Take your family on an unforgettable experience with activities like a guided boat tour of the area, a river cruise, and a sampan ride. Along the route to the river, you may pass hundreds of temples, tombs, flower fields, and rice paper manufacturers in addition to the breathtaking scenery.

Dong Thap province's Tram Chim National Park is home to around 200 different species of birds, some of which are uncommon. Your family may go bird watching there to learn about the ecology and provide the kids an excellent opportunity to learn about animals.

Vietnam and Cambodia travel guide 2023-2024

Scan code for major destinations in Vietnam

BUDGET FOR CAMBODIA

Traveling to Cambodia is quite inexpensive, especially when compared to other South East Asian travel destinations.

Make accommodations
A decent hotel room should cost at least $60 USD (£46) and a pleasant guesthouse room should cost at least $30 USD (£23).
For as little as $4 USD (£3) per night, backpacker hostels provide dorm rooms; but, if you're traveling in a pair, a private room may be had for as little as $10 USD (£7.60).

Meals
Cambodian food is cheap, especially from street food sellers. lunches may cost as little as $1–2 USD (75p–£1.50), while basic lunches in neighborhood eateries run from $3–5 USD (£2.30-£3.80). You should budget a bit extra for dining in establishments

targeted towards visitors, between $5–$15 USD (£3.80-£11.40) per person.

Move around

The most economical method to travel about is to use the local public transportation system. Although they are incredibly inexpensive and simple to hail, always double-check the fare before getting in. Additionally, you may hire a driver to pick you up and drop you off at an attraction or for the duration of the day.

Since buses link larger towns or places, they are slightly more expensive. The approximate cost of a bus ticket from Phnom Penh to Siem Reap is $10 USD (£7.60 GBP) per person.

Highlights

The majority of attractions have affordable admission fees; one such example is the Choeung Ek Killing Fields in Phnom Penh, which only costs $5 USD (£3.80). But you must budget for the relatively high admission fees to Angkor Wat while planning your trip.

One-day ($37/£28), three-day ($62/£47), and seven-day ($72/£55) passes are available for purchase. Although they must be used within a certain time limit, they are not required to be used on consecutive days. The three-day permit, for instance, must be used within ten days.

❖ Places to Go in Cambodia

➢ Hanoi, Ph.

Once you cross the border from southern Laos into Cambodia, Phnom Penh, the country's capital, is among the most fascinating destinations to see. Despite its historical significance, Phnom Penh has a charming riverbank atmosphere due to its proximity to the Mekong.

To fully comprehend Cambodia's horrific past, visitors must absorb the horrific history in the Choeung Ek Killing Fields and the Tuol Sleng Genocide Museum. Sadly, not many people are aware of the tale told by these two websites.

While seeing Phnom Penh, it is also highly recommended that you stop by the stunning Royal Palace, which is close to the city center. Since the 1860s, the majestic gardens have been home to the Kings of Cambodia.

Apart from its primary tourist destinations, Phnom Penh has several marketplaces where you can get anything from jewelry to leggings to seafood and anything in between. While the Phnom Penh night market is a terrific spot to stop by for some dinner at night, the Russian Market is a great place to buy for anything and everything. The most common mode of transportation in the city, the tuk-tuk, is the best method to travel to both. This trip is a fantastic way to see Wat Phnom Temple, the Russian Market, and the National Museum all at once.

Another well-known feature of Phnom Penh is the abundance of Happy Pizza parlors, which serve standard pizza with a whimsical twist of "happy" toppings. These stores are typically located close to the riverbank that runs beside the Mekong.

> ### Choeung Ek Death Zones

Another moving reminder of Cambodia's sad past—the country was ruled by the Khmer Rouge from 1975 to 1979—is the Choeung Ek Killing Fields. The notorious killing fields in Cambodia claimed the lives of millions of people due to malnutrition, excessive labor, or premeditated killings. The Choeung Ek

Killing Fields, located outside of Phnom Penh's city, are among the most well-known.

You may be asking yourself why someone would travel to such a horrific location where many defenseless men, women, and children suffered excruciating agony before passing away. But for a very specific reason, this terrifying location has to be at the top of your list if you're ever in Phnom Penh: while history books can tell you about the atrocities committed in the past, you can only truly understand their scope by going to the scene and hearing the testimonies of the victims.

Although it is undoubtedly an emotional event, it is important to honor the victims' lives and learn for the future. Experiencing the numerous skulls, mass graves, and torture sites alongside an extremely educational audio commentary is guaranteed to be one of your most enlightening experiences ever.

It is rather simple to go from Phnom Penh to the Choeung Ek Killing Fields. For a nominal charge, you may take a tuk tuk for the half-hour ride, and your driver will drop you off at the gate. Recognize that, as a sign of respect for the victims, you have to wear modest clothing. Additionally, bear in mind that minors are not advised to participate in this strenuous event.

➢ **Reap Siem**

Nobody visits Siem Reap whilst in Cambodia without doing so. Siem Reap, the home of famous temples like Angkor Wat, is a well-liked stop on any itinerary through South East Asia.

There are several additional sights, such the Cambodian Land Mine Museum and the floating town of Kompong Phluk, to keep you occupied while you're not temple touring. With lovely canals crisscrossing the city, Siem Reap is a lovely destination to spend a few days in. It's undoubtedly much less hectic than Phnom Penh. The city's business hub is the unimaginatively called Pub Street. There's a distinct Khao San atmosphere to it at night, but during the day there are many of great eateries for breakfast and lunch, many with lovely, sun-filled patios. In the evening, don't forget to visit one of the top-notch French eateries or visit the Old Market to try some of the regional street cuisine. Wat Bo Road, a neighborhood not far from Pub Street, is another developing district with a vibrant mix of eateries and pubs. An additional option would be to attend a Khmer cooking lesson to better understand the food or get tickets to the Apsara Theatre to see a performance of a traditional dance.

Accommodations in Siem Reap

If you want to see Angkor Wat before dawn, you'll probably be on the go for the most of your stay in Siem Reap, including some extremely early beginnings.

Having said that, I advise choosing a location that is very calm and cozy because there is a lot to do in Siem Reap both during the day and at night. You'll need a place to rest after a long day of touring and wandering. A dorm room is not what I advise!

The Park Hyatt Siem Reap (£77 per night), Anantara Resort & Spa (£80 per night), and Shinta Mani Shack (£153 per night) are a few of the nicest places to stay in luxury.

Try Belmond La Résidence d'Angkor (£148 per night) for an extravagant stay.

Templation (£68 per night) and Navutu Dreams Resort (£48 per night) are excellent choices for the finest mid-range accommodations.

On the other hand, One Stop Hostel on Pub Street is a great option if you want a vibrant hostel experience. If you're looking for a reasonably priced haven, consider Bokre Angkor Hostel.

➤ **Angkor Thom**

A visit to the Angkor Wat temple complex is a must-do when visiting Cambodia. The most important monument in the nation, Angkor Wat welcomes almost half a million tourists annually. With an expansive 400 acres of land, Angkor Wat is the greatest religious monument in the whole globe. For numerous centuries, it served as the epicenter of the formidable Khmer kingdom. With up to 750,000 residents living inside the complex, Angkor Wat was the most spectacular and sophisticated metropolis in the world at the time.

The temple was constructed in the twelfth century. The sandstone stones needed to construct Angkor Wat were transported down the Siem Reap River on rafts, a journey of more than 50 kilometers. An estimated 300,000 laborers and 6000 elephants were used in the building of the temple complex. and it received the UNESCO World Heritage Site designation in the 1990s. There are a few explanations as to why Angkor Wat was abandoned, and the surrounding forest eventually reclaimed the temple complex. Later, European explorers "rediscovered" it, and ever since, South East Asia has made it a major tourist destination.

The largest and most striking temple is the main one. It is most beautiful at sunrise or dusk when the surrounding lake reflects the spires, creating a mystical atmosphere.

About 7 kilometers separate Angkor Wat from Siem Reap, which offers a great selection of lodging options. Seeing Angkor Wat with a local guide is highly recommended since they may provide you with more knowledge on the temples' significance and history, allowing you to fully appreciate what you're seeing!

The cost of a one-day admission to enter the temple complex is USD $37 (£28), as was previously noted in the budget section. Every day from 5 am to 6 pm, the park is open.

Taking a guided tour is another option to see Angkor Wat. Numerous alternatives are available, most of which are best explored in small groups with an experienced local guide who can show you around each temple.

> **Hey Prohm**

The Ta Prohm temple, which is also near Siem Reap, is a remarkable site that is definitely worth seeing.

Constructed in the 13th century as a Buddhist monastery in the Bayon style, it was dedicated to King Jayavarman VII's mother. Today, visiting it is like going on a true adventure since the forest has totally taken over the remains.

Ta Prohm is unique in that its most noticeable feature is the trees that sprout out of the remains, which has made it a famous tourist destination. The temple gained international recognition after appearing in Angelina Jolie's Tomb Raider film in 2001. As a result, the temple was given the moniker Tomb Raider Temple in the west. You can investigate the temple's enclosed courtyard and cramped hallways. Due to the roots of the trees pushing aside some of the stone barriers that limit particular locations, some of the passageways are inaccessible. The temple is a dark and gloomy location to explore, with towering trees filtering the sunlight and moss, crawling vines, and shrub shoots decorating the walls.

The Angkor Wat entry pass includes admission to Ta Prohm, although individual and small group trips are also available, which include transportation from Siem Reap.

At Angkor Thom, the Bayon Temple

One of the numerous temples in the Angkor Thom complex, Bayon is among the top tourist destinations in Cambodia. Huge stone faces that are smiling on its towers make it easy to recognize. One of the most significant of all the temples in the Angkor Thom complex, Bayon Temple was built during the period when Angkor was the capital of the Khmer Kingdom, in the late 13th century. When viewed from a distance, Bayon resembles a straightforward temple made of grey stone, but up close, the 216 faces become more visible.

Some claim that the faces are those of King Jayavarman Vll, who was dressed like a god throughout his rule. Some claim to be of the Buddhist bodhisattva of Compassion, Lokesvara. Through the maze-like corridors of Bayon, it seems as though the four towers' four 4-meter-tall faces are staring down at you from every direction. You are transported back over 900 years by the temple's decaying interior, exquisite stone sculptures, and joyful stone faces. At that time, the World Heritage Site-worthy Angkor Thom's walled city was home to this magnificent Buddhist temple. Today, tourists swarm to the region attracted by the allure of Angkor Thom's vanished civilization and abandoned remains recovered by Mother Nature. When the sun is sinking and the throng have dispersed in the late afternoon, get out; you could have Bayon all to yourself. At that point, you'll understand why this temple ranks among the most amazing sites in all of Cambodia.

➢ **Si Banteay**

Just 37 meters separate Banteay Srei, often known as the "Citadel of Women," from Siem Reap. Even though Banteay Srei is farther out from the city than Angkor Wat, it nonetheless sees a good number of tourists. One may easily spend a half-day visiting the location as the tuk-tuk ride takes around one hour each way. Plan to come as soon as the temple door opens, if at all possible. Please be aware that this excursion requires an Angkor pass, which will be punched if it is a brand-new day.

Because the grounds are not large, you will have more time to examine the elaborate reliefs and statues. Compared to other parts of Angkor, the sculptures here are more detailed. That's why folks who called them Banteay Srei thought they could only have been made by women's delicate fingers. These epic-retelling sculptures abound on the doorframes, lintels, and archways of the inner shrines. You can visit the site in an hour or so, but by then the tour buses would have come to unload the crowds.

On the way back, the trip to Banteay Srei usually includes a stop at the Cambodia Landmine Museum. Ask your driver to stop for a bowl of num ban chok near the Preah Dak intersection if you're hungry. This is a meal of flavorful noodles served with chicken, blood curd, and fresh herbs in a somewhat spicy stew. It's really nourishing and delicious!

➤ **Museum of Landmines in Cambodia**

The Cambodian Land Mine Museum is another fascinating place to go. It's only a quick tuk-tuk journey outside of Siem Reap.

Aki Ra was a Khmer Rouge soldier when he first founded the museum. He planted land mines all throughout Cambodia as part of his job. Aki now chooses to dedicate much of his time to neutralizing detonated land mines as an act of contrition. This is now what he views as his life's work. He has actually discovered a large number of the landmines and explosives in the museum. His job is vital because unexploded landmines still kill dozens of Cambodians year. Although millions have been removed, the nation regrettably continues to rank among the most severely land-mined in the world.

The struggle that lasted for decades led to this. American bombardment, a civil war, the Vietnamese occupation, and the terrible Khmer Rouge rule.

Taking a stroll through the museum evokes strong feelings. Despite being a small museum, there is a ton of information available. Information regarding the Khmer Rouge and the crimes they carried out in Cambodia is kept in a few rooms. However, locating and neutralizing land mines is the primary priority. There's also a section that simulates the appearance of Khmer Rouge soldiers.

Adult admission is $5 (£3.80), while children under 10 enter free of charge. It is an experience you should not miss if you are in Siem Reap.

Cambodia's east
> **Kratie**

The town of Kratié is located on the banks of the Mekong River in eastern Cambodia. Situated a full 240 kilometers north of bustling Phnom Penh, it's an ideal spot to spend a few days relaxing and taking in rural Cambodia.

The Irrawaddy dolphins are without a doubt Kratié's main attraction. These river dolphins belong to a species that may be found in parts of South Asia's Mekong, especially in Cambodia and Laos. Their facial features are similar to those of beluga whales, with a rounded, flat face and a mouth that seems to open in a smile. They have acquired the endearing moniker "the smiling face of The Mekong" as a result. Kratié is a great place to start your journey to see the Irrawaddy dolphins since there is a pod of around 20 of them in the Mekong, only 11km north of the hamlet in Kampi.

I suggest picking up a motorbike or bicycle from Kratié and riding it to Kampi. There should be a cluster of yellow boats waiting near the bank as you approach Kampi. These are standing by to take visitors out onto the river to look for dolphins. You have a good chance of seeing dolphins because the knowledgeable boatmen are aware of their specific locations. The greatest times to visit, though, are in the early morning or late afternoon when the dolphins are usually most active. The toughest issue is trying to obtain a picture of them because they only appear for a short while!

➢ Murderous Cavities in Battambang

You have time to think about your impending visit as you ride the rough tuk-tuk out to the Killing Caves. The Phnom Sampov mountains are a tiny range of mountains located immediately outside Battambang town. People were taken here by Khmer Rouge members who had mercilessly murdered them after tearing them apart for their families. It is really painful to think about the horrors that occurred at these caverns.

You will be dropped off at a tiny village at the foot of the hills so you may see these caverns. From here, hiking to the peak—where the caverns are located—takes about an hour. To reach the summit, you may also get in a 4x4 with a local driver. This alternative just requires fifteen minutes. A sequence of caverns on Phnom Sampeau, one of the mountains, lead to larger caverns deeper down the shaft. The victim was shoved into the shaft that descended into the cave after being beaten or struck in the head at the top. A few victims were simply shoved down the shaft and allowed to fall to their deaths. A monument to the victims of the Khmer dictatorship is currently located in the bigger of the caverns. Skulls of some of the

10,000 victims from the cave are on display at a monument.

Scan for places to go in Cambodia

Vietnam and Cambodia travel guide 2023-2024

CULTURE AND TRADITIONS

❖ Vietnamese Heritage & Culture

Vietnam's culture is a synthesis of French, Chinese, and neighboring Cambodian civilizations. Vietnam is in Southeast Asia, but it was ruled by China for a long time, thus the cultures of the two countries are remarkably similar. Because of this, it is mostly thought of as a melting pot of immigrants from China, Japan, Taiwan, and Korea. Later, the Vietnamese overlords took over further Khmer regime components, absorbing aspects of Cambodian culture in the process. The adoption of the Latin alphabet, the growth of Catholicism, and the predominance of bread and pastries in Vietnamese cuisine are other indications of the French colonial impact.

Vietnamese religions

Taoism, Buddhism, and Confucianism are the three main faiths practiced by the majority of Vietnamese people. The populace worships their ancestors as well. Ancestral altars are typically found in homes and businesses. Vietnam boasts a number of Buddhist and Confucianist temples, including the Thein Mu Pagoda, Perfume Pagoda, and Bai Dinh Pagoda, as evidence of this tradition. But again, the Cao Dai Temple is unique. People from different religious backgrounds participate actively in its festivities, and it views all religions equally. The effect of French colonization has also led to an increase in the number of persons who practice Catholicism. The French-imported bricks used to build Ho Chi Minh City's Notre-Dame Basilica are evidence of the colonists' attempts to spread Christianity across Vietnam. A few Hindu temples may also be found in Vietnam, such as the Mariamman Temple, which is well-liked by the minority Hindu Chams tribe and is thought to have been founded by Hindu traders.

Vietnam's Traditional Clothes

Throughout history, Vietnam's traditional attire has experienced several transformations due to the influence of multiple dynasties. On the other hand, the Ao Dai has endured over time. The ao dai was originally worn by both sexes, but it is now mostly associated with women. These days, Vietnamese fashion is dominated by Western attire, with the Ao Dai only being worn on special occasions or as part of the work and school uniform. The Non-La, a conical hat that has come to symbolize Vietnam, is another example of traditional Vietnamese clothing. When visiting Vietnam, do not forget to purchase the authentic Ao Dai and Non-La! Ao Dais are priced at VND 500,000, but the Non-La is only available for VND 25,000!

Languages in Vietnam

Chinese has had a significant impact on the dominant language, Vietnamese. Owing to their colonial history, France, Russia, and England have also left their marks (owing to the respective belligerent armies during the Vietnam War). The several ethnic communities in this area speak Tay, Khmer, Muong, and Cham in addition to Vietnamese. French and

Chinese are among the foreign languages that are also understood.

Since many individuals in Vietnam's cities speak English fluently, travelers may not encounter many language barriers while there. If, however, you intend to visit rural parts of Vietnam, you may encounter an issue.

Vietnamese Art Forms:

1. Literature

Vietnamese literature mostly falls into two categories: written and folk. Vietnamese folklore comprises fables, fairy tales, myths, folk music, and poetry that are deeply ingrained in the culture of the people. The fundamental themes of folk literature were moral qualities, humanism, and the appreciation of nature's beauty. On the other side, the written literature, which includes plays, poetry, and novels, was greatly impacted by the Chinese language. Modern literature has explored combat and depicted the ordinary lives of individuals in Vietnam, ranging from romanticism to realism.If you have an interest in literature, you should make time on your agenda to visit the Vietnam Literature Museum and the Temple of Literature, which are both located in Hanoi and are home to Vietnam's first university, The Imperial Academy.

2. *Painting with Silk*

Vietnam's silk paintings are well-known. Although silk paintings are popular in China and other East Asian nations, Vietnamese silk paintings stand out due to its French influences and bold color choices. Typically, these paintings depict Vietnamese daily life.

Cutting-Out Painting

Vietnamese Dong Ho woodblock prints are created by slicing complex patterns into wood, coating it with natural pigments, and then pressing it on paper. Recently, this art style has also become more well-known outside of Vietnam. Since woodblock paintings are frequently purchased during the Lunar New Year, topics like luck, well-known tales, and daily life are shown in vivid colors to evoke hope for the next year.

During the Lunar New Year vacation, you may visit the Dong Ho village to partake in a painting festival and purchase one as a memento!

Arts and Performance in Vietnam

Dances from Vietnam
An essential component of Vietnamese culture is dance. Every ethnic group has a unique style of dancing. Traditional dances are those that are done at opera houses, theaters, festivals, and the former royal court. Festivals feature the popular Lion Dance, which is meant to fend off evil spirits. The Lantern dancing, Fan Dance, Lotus Dance, and Ribbon Dance are some further Vietnamese dancing styles.

Vietnam Music
It is impossible to separate Vietnamese music from dance and theater. The rich history of this song dates back to the Nguyen dynasty. Vietnam has around fifty native musical instruments, including wind, percussion, and string instruments that are widely employed in different artistic genres. Vietnam's music primarily consists of three genres: Ca Tru, a type of chamber music that UNESCO has designated as an intangible cultural treasure; imperial music played as a ritual at the royal courts; and folk music, the style of which progressively varies with the area. At the Phuong Bao Music Centre in Ho Chi Minh City, you may take in a traditional Vietnamese dance

and music performance accompanied by tea and sweets. The range of ticket pricing is from VND 320,000 to VND 380,000.

Vietnamese Martial Arts
Though not as well-known as its Chinese or Japanese equivalents, Vietnamese martial arts are becoming more and more well-known worldwide. Despite having a lot of Chinese martial arts influence, the martial art is nonetheless rather unique. It is a very spiritual practice with Taoist and Buddhist ideas at its core. The Vietnamese call it Vo Thuat, and it's mainly known for its scissor kicks.

Vietnam's Water Puppetry
The art form known as Mua Roi has been recognized by UNESCO as an intangible cultural treasure. It features vibrantly colored wooden puppets that are submerged in water and controlled with long poles beneath the water stage, displaying the many national customs.
At the Golden Dragon Water Puppet Theatre in Ho Chi Minh City, a water puppet performance is available for just under VND 230,000.

Vietnamese cuisine

Vietnamese cuisine is highly healthful and holds great cultural significance, much like its art forms. The cuisine is made to incorporate all five basic flavors and important nutrients while also appealing to the body's five senses. The cuisine makes liberal use of fresh meats, veggies, and herbs. Their cuisine is likewise heavily influenced by France. The majority of recipes have a broth or noodle basis and are visually pleasing since they are colorful. Since rice is more frequently consumed than wheat, the cuisine also utilizes relatively little oil, dairy, and gluten.

Pho, Goi Cuon, Com Tam, and the renowned Banh Mi are all must-try foods!

Vietnamese Holidays and Festivities

Vietnam celebrates a number of holidays with great fanfare and grandeur, the two most well-known being Tet (Lunar New Year) and Tet Trung Thu (Lantern Festival). With a plethora of events and fireworks, Hanoi offers the ultimate Lunar New Year experience. As a harvest celebration, Tet Trung Thu is vibrant, with people assembling to light lanterns. On this day, the lion dance is also performed. Reunification Day and Independence Day are additional holidays observed in Vietnam, marked by parades and other events.

❖ Vietnam's Dos and Don'ts of Etiquette

It is customary to engage in some small conversation with people before addressing the topic at hand.

While it is customary to witness two friends of the same sex holding hands, it is best to refrain from making public shows of affection toward those of the other sex.

In Vietnam, crossing one's fingers for good fortune is considered an impolite gesture.

Use both hands while giving something to someone who is older than you.

Make a hand motion instead of pointing with your finger.

When you go inside someone's house, take off your shoes.

The Vietnamese Temple Etiquette

Before you enter a temple, take off your shoes and hat.
Dress modestly; avoid shorts, bare midriffs, and exposed shoulders.
Never turn your back on a statue or image of Buddha.
Avoid smoking.
Prior to shooting pictures, ask.

Vietnam Food and Socialization

Bring candies, flowers, or fruits when you are invited into someone's house, but don't give four of anything—that is an unlucky number. At weddings, cash in an envelope is always appreciated, but gifts of wine and spirits are also suitable.
They use chopsticks in Vietnam. Another typical spoon for soups and broths is a flat one.
Your chopsticks should never be placed point-down in a dish; instead, place them on the top of the table.
Family-style meals often consist of many main courses, rice or noodles, and a clear broth for dessert. Meat, fish, and vegetables are frequently served over rice in bowls.

The eldest member of the group takes a seat first and starts the meal.

In restaurants, the check is only given out once the head of the table asks for it and everyone has finished. Vietnamese eating culture does not practice separate checks; instead, it is customary to offer to split the bill after the dinner.

Give the cashier or wait staff your money in person whenever you can.

Tipping is always appreciated but is not necessary. Tipping about 10% or rounding up the check is becoming more and more usual.

Vietnam's Business Etiquette and Customs

It's common practice to present and receive business cards using both hands. Vietnamese businesspeople almost never go without a card.

Men greet one other with a polite handshake before entering and leaving a business meeting.

Vietnamese women are not always willing to shake hands, especially with men. In such a situation, a modest, polite bow is in order.

Establishing contacts through small chat and socializing beforehand is crucial while conducting business in Vietnam.

Refrain from confronting someone; it is better to remain silent than to argue openly and risk seeming foolish.

Many Vietnamese people will avoid making direct eye contact; this is done out of regard to the speaker and not as a show of disdain or indifference.

Vietnam and Cambodia travel guide 2023-2024

CAMBODIAN CULTURE AND TRADITIONS

People from all over the world come to the borders of Cambodia to see its fascinating culture firsthand. You can see, feel, and experience so much in Cambodia—from the temples to the historical landmarks to the gentle smiles on the cheeks of young monks. It is estimated that the Khmer people's ancestors arrived in the Angkor region between 5,000 and 10,000 years ago. They find themselves on Tonle Sap Lake's shoreline due to excellent fishing. It is believed that the Khmers and Indians first interacted in the year AD. 100, when merchants searched for a sea passage to China so they could conduct business. Since then, the animistic Khmer culture has adapted to Buddhism, which has led to the development of the culture into what it is today: an incredibly spiritual and unique way of existing in the world.

The primary ideals of Cambodia

Cambodia is a country where customs are both strikingly similar to and far distinct from those of the West. In both cultures, family, religion, and different customs are significant. The way these principles are demonstrated, nevertheless, differs greatly from the customs and ways of life in each of the other planets.

kin

In this culture, family and providing for that family are very important. It's interesting to note that links to people beyond the family are also highly valued, as are obligations to the community. In fact, these obligations are taken so seriously that they are comparable to those made to one's own family.

Tempo

Most people in Cambodia come from rural backgrounds. The way that Cambodians relate to time has changed significantly because they do not have the time constraints and never-ending demands that we in the West have grown so accustomed to. People are more event-oriented than temporally focused. This implies that lunch will be served in line with the day's events rather than when you decide to eat it based on the time on your watch. It will happen later or early depending on the situation. It's easier for things to happen more naturally and instinctively when they aren't scheduled.

Partnerships

Interpersonal interactions are highly valued by the people of Cambodia. One's time priorities are determined by their interactions with others, which is such an intriguing idea! The requirements of others and one's connection with them take precedence above one's own loyalty and priorities, which are not based on our own wants.

Lethargic thinking

Additionally, Cambodians have a fatalistic attitude on life and a sense of diminished accountability. It is harder to change the path of life or improve one's chances by acting on behalf of oneself. People frequently accept their circumstances and learn to live with them. Although this is a bitter pill to chew for nations that value ambition and enterprise, who is to tell which perspective is better for your wellbeing?

❖ Customary gender roles for men and women

The horrifying Khmer Rouge left an irreversible mark on the composition of the nuclear family in Cambodia. Millions of family members perished during this period, leaving an astounding number of families without two parents and without enough adult companionship to manage home matters.

Due to the high number of families who perished during the Khmer Rouge era, a household may have a diverse variety of related combinations. Families with only one parent that are headed by a widow are not uncommon. Household members frequently share resources, labor, and food.

The husband is the Khmer family's legal head. The husband is responsible for providing food and shelter for the family, as was the strict law in the past in the Western world. This is a difficult duty to bear! In addition, males and husbands are in charge of labor-intensive physical jobs including threshing rice, harrowing and plowing rice paddies, and tending to animals. They are also supposed to handle any carpentry requirements. No, not easy again. At least they won't have to deal with malfunctioning WiFi, IT issues, or the ramifications of a teenage girl running amok in a mall.

The nation is rife with misogyny and has a blatant double standard, particularly in the more rural areas of the nation. With at least ten years of education under their belts, men are often much better educated. Conversely, women have a glaring lack of education; just 16 percent of females in the nation are enrolled in school. Although the country's salaries may not be enough, it is true that just around 6% of women receive compensation for their labor.

Because of this, a wife's or woman's function seldom extends outside the home. Thousands of women in Cambodia have been compelled to assume extraordinary strength as a result of the atrocities committed by the Khmer Rouge, taking on tasks that a household with more than one parent would typically share. The same labor-intensive tasks that males do are frequently carried out by women. Women will work in the fields, create other items, engage in trade and exchanges, and handle household chores like laundry and housekeeping. It truly is a marvel that single mothers can manage everything; it is evidence of the resilience of the human spirit. The spiritual leaders of the household are women as well.

They point them in the direction of the light and mentor and teach them about religion and ethics.

❖ Traditional ideas and religion

It is said that the merchants who sailed via the Gulf of Thailand on their route to China had a significant effect on Cambodian religion. It is believed that Indian culture was brought to the region up until the Funan Kingdom of the time first absorbed its religious practices.

Buddhism-

As a result, the nation, like the entirety of South East Asia, has a sizable Buddhist population. Buddhists who practice Theravada Buddhism make up around 90% of the people in Cambodia. It is a non-prescriptive, tolerant religion that does not need belief in a higher power.

Indian

Around the same time as Buddhism, Hinduism made its way into Cambodia. It was and remains one of the state's recognized faiths. In actuality, Angkor Wat is the world's biggest Hindu temple!

Islam.

Another recognized religion in the Kingdom is Islam. During the Khmer Rouge, the number of practicing

Muslims was so drastically reduced as to unite the many religious factions. Even now, a sizable section of the population travels to Malaysia to study the Qur'an, and some even go on pilgrimages to Mecca.

Faithfulness In the nation, Christianity is essentially nonexistent. Some 2000 individuals were converted by small missionary centers in Battambang and Siem Riep in the early 1960s. Although Buddhism predominates in the nation, other religions are also recognized in Cambodia, as are their customs, buildings, and adherents' integrity. The reason for this is that Buddhism is a highly welcoming and tolerant religion.

Architecture & Arts

The arts of Cambodia have been led and motivated by religious ideals throughout its turbulent and adventurous past.

The fusion of the native animistic beliefs and the Buddhism religion, which was originally practiced in India, produced the distinctive Khmer style that is displayed in wats and museums. Since this first cultural melting pot thousands of years ago, incredibly magnificent art and architecture have been created.

The religious ideas that underlie a sculpture or other work of art are quite clear to see. The sculptures possess an air of acceptance, elegance, grace, and beauty that the people of Cambodia really cherish. The nation is filled with several specimens of Khmer sculpture. The aesthetic is calming and captivating. Hindu deities are frequently portrayed with a high degree of skill and flair. Spend some time truly absorbing them!

There aren't many differences between the dwellings of the ancient Khmers and the communities of contemporary Cambodia. Homes were mostly made of wood and were situated rather high above the ground. The roof was covered with coconut palms or thatched leaves, and the walls were constructed of bamboo. Remarkably, architecture and ornamentation reflect socioeconomic position, much as they do in the West. Impressive structures of days are more a sign of riches than of social or political influence. On the other hand, the different types of residences in Cambodia's rural areas are associated with the families' socioeconomic status. The residences of dignitaries were larger, made of sturdy wood, and had tile roofs. Making residences that resembled those of a class higher than one's own was considered unthinkable due to the sheer nature of its incompatibility with one's own social position, rather than just being beyond the means of the average person.

Conventional attire

Being able to wear traditional clothing on a daily basis is quite unique. The traditional clothing of Cambodia is worn all year round, unlike the Scottish kilt that is decorated for a wedding just once a year. Several times a year, people will wear special, occasion-specific attire that is easy to spot thanks to its vibrant colors and detailed patterns. The majority of the traditional clothing is fashioned from golden silk with Cambodian-only patterns and decorations.

There are a few items that people wear on a daily basis in addition to the classy and colorful traditional attire; some are so practical that you won't be impressed by your jeans' one-use only. More useful than a Leatherman, a karma is a thin piece of fabric the size of a towel. They are frequently used as sarongs, to carry items inside, and to drape over people's heads to shade them from the sun. They're even used as accessories for fashion! Hey! How varied a situation may be.

The Sampot is the Kingdom's national attire. Wearers of this style of sarong, both men and women, make an impression on fellow travelers who are ill-prepared, hot, and uncomfortable.

Customary dance
In Cambodia, dance is a highly esteemed art form. Cambodia is claimed to have been founded between a celestial dancer and a monarch. As one might expect, dancing is very common throughout the Kingdom. Dancers are frequently emblazoned on large posters; you may see them at performances, on the walls of Angor Wat, and even in the streets. The nation has three different types of dances. Classical, religious, and folk. Out of the three, classical dance is currently the most popular in the nation. The demands of contemporary entertainment and the declining degree of tradition transmission from generation to generation must be combated through the art form.

Traditional cuisine
The staples of traditional Cambodian cuisine are noodles, soups, curries, and an assortment of fried and grilled foodstuffs.
Paste-making is a specialty of the Cambodian people. Fresh components and a mysterious procedure

(reasonable assumption) combine to provide a product that is far superior than the sum of its parts. The most widely used components are prawn and fish pastes. You'll discover that there will be some in or on your table whether you buy Fish Amok or grilled crab at the waterfront! This will make you extremely pleased very soon.

Customary festivities

There are so many amazing festivals in Cambodia that visiting the nation only for those events would be worthwhile. The Khmer New Year is one of the most widely observed. Three days of festivities line the streets of the major cities in the first few days of April. Everybody has a hopeful, grateful expression on their face, and their homes are beautifully adorned. Their faces also have a significant layer of talcum powder on them. Another unique celebration is the water festival. For this one, make sure you're in the Phnom Penh area around late October. Celebrate in style the Mekong River's changing of the tide and all that it has made possible for the people of Cambodia.

❖ Cambodian Manners and Etiquette

Meet and Salute

The way that individuals greet each other in Cambodia is influenced by their age, connection, and social status.

It is customary to welcome the oldest or most senior person first and the youngest or least senior person last.

Approaching the person at the bottom of the hierarchy directly might make the senior member of the group feel embarrassed.

A bow and a chest-level raising of the hands—akin to lifting them in prayer—combine to form the customary welcome.

The hands are raised and the bow is lowered when one wants to demonstrate deeper respect.

Cambodians have embraced the western custom of shaking hands when they meet outsiders.

Women are still allowed to welcome people in Cambodia traditionally.

The simplest guideline is to return the favor by welcoming someone.

The honorific titles "Lok" for men and "Lok Srey" for women are used to address persons in Cambodia.

This is followed by either the first name alone or the first and surname together.

Etiquette for Giving Gifts
At the Cambodian New Year (Chaul Chnam), gifts are typically exchanged.
Unlike in the West, birthdays are rarely a huge deal, and many elderly individuals might not even know when they were born.
The majority of other civilizations do not observe birthdays, including Cambodians. In actuality, a lot of elderly folks might not be aware of their own birthdate.
You can also accept a little gift if you are invited to eat at someone's house.
When visiting someone's house, bring beautifully arranged fruit, candies, pastries, or flowers.
Don't offer knives.
Typically, gifts are wrapped in vibrant paper.
Avoid using white wrapping paper since that hue is associated with grief.
Give gifts with both hands.
Presents are not unwrapped right away.

Dining Protocols

Table etiquette is largely formal.

Generally, Cambodians use a spoon and fork or chopsticks while they eat.

When kids use a fork and spoon, they transfer food onto the spoon with the fork before putting the spoon in their mouth.

Additionally, it's not unusual for Cambodians to eat with their hands.

Simply copy what others do if you're unsure about the dos and don'ts.

You should not disturb any hierarchical arrangements by waiting to be directed where to seat when you are called to the dinner table.

Typically, the oldest individual is seated first.

In a similar vein, the oldest individual ought to eat first.

Wait until the oldest person starts eating before you start.

Never talk business in these kinds of social situations.

Cambodian Business Etiquette and Culture
Meet and Salutations

Given that Cambodian society is hierarchical, business practices and conventions in the region mirror this.

The older individual must always be treated with regard and respect.

As the most senior member of your group will present you to the group's top-ranking member, you should do the same.

When there are groups engaged, you should present individuals according on their rank so that your colleagues in Cambodia are aware of the dynamics inside the group.

Shaking hands is customary, however take care not to be overly forceful since this might be interpreted as hostile.

Men should wait to aid women until after they have extended one. Minimize eye contact as much as possible.

When addressing someone by their first name alone or by combining their first and surname, Cambodians use the honorific "Lok" for men and "Lok Srey" for women.

Meetings for Business

In Cambodia, time is not as valuable as it is in other societies. Meetings thus don't always follow an agenda or timetable.

Meetings can be a little bit cyclical, so problems can be discussed independently and collectively if necessary. Also, if a problem appears to be fixed, it might come up again later.

Meetings will go on until all participants believe the topic has been adequately covered.

It is important to establish a connection based on mutual trust, so take the time to get to know your opponents at first.

Meetings should always start with a little small conversation.

Because Cambodians communicate in highly indirect ways, it's important to be able to read between the lines.

They constantly think through the ramifications of their words and comments, especially if they are unpleasant and raise face-saving concerns. In fact, if Cambodians disagree with someone, they would prefer to keep quiet than say something that may annoy or humiliate someone else in the room.

You could think that you are not receiving a clear response because of the indirect nature of Cambodian communication and the importance put on appearances.

This might be the case if your Cambodian coworker feels uncomfortable with a proposed course of action or disagrees with you but is reluctant to express it. You should try to learn more about their genuine emotions by posing a variety of open-ended questions.

The preference of the Cambodian people is to wait for others to react before voicing opinions.

A genuine turn-off is speech that is forceful, strained, or pompous.

Being on time is essential. Being late for an appointment demonstrates your lack of consideration for the other person.

Recognizing nonverbal cues is as crucial. For instance, smiling in Cambodia is situational and can convey a variety of emotions, such as nervousness, irritation, or even a lack of understanding of what has been stated.

Emotional expression is viewed as a bad behavior. It is best to keep feelings of rage, irritation, or annoyance inside since they might cause embarrassment.

openly is seen as a show of weakness and bad manners and is not part of the culture.

Since the culture places a high value on modesty and humility, praises and appreciation are typically met with disparaging remarks.
Speaking with bluster is not a good idea since it might be taken as boasting.
Stay out of extended eye contact.
Make sure you talk slowly and clearly, and refrain from using slang, proverbs, or colloquial expressions.

Shopping
Phnom Penh's marketplaces provide a wide variety of intriguing and handcrafted goods for purchase. For instance, Cambodians use checkered fabric, known as Krama, as a belt, turban, or scarf. Traditionally, they are made in red and white or blue and white, but modern weavers use a variety of colors. The most exquisite kramas are from Kampong Cham and are made entirely of silk or cotton. Among the many other things for sale are stalls with silver jewelry, wooden carvings, copper artifacts, paintings, and sculptures of historical prints. One bazaar in Phnom Penh that tourists should not miss is the Russian market, which is filled with inexpensive branded apparel and trinkets. It is highly banned to take Khmer antiques out of the country. Avoid bringing in sculptures from bogus merchants or stones you found

in temples; the customs officers at Siem Reap International Airport are trained to spot these things.

Sip
Steer clear of tap water (and ice) and only use bottled mineral water, making sure the cap is still in place. There are many of carbonated beverages available for purchase, along with light, blonde beer (Angkor is the preferred bottle). Tea, especially jasmine tea, is served at all eateries. Strong, sugary coffee is blended with condensed milk. Fresh juices are sold from stands along the street, but be careful—they might upset your stomach.

Official language
Khméré
Spoken languages
85% of people in Cambodia speak Khmer, a non-tonal language with a written alphabet based on the Pallava script of southern India that is uncommon in the area. Chinese, Vietnamese, and Cham are the main minority languages. English is the second most common foreign language spoken (spoken by 5% of speakers), behind French (15%).
Persons

Of all Cambodians, 85.4% are Khmers. There are only 7.4% Vietnamese, 3.5% Cham, 3.2% Chinese, 0.2% Kui, and 0.2% Mnong. The Central Plains are home to the Khmer, Vietnamese, and Chinese; the mountainous regions are inhabited by the Cham, Kui, Mnong, and other ancient tribes.

Holiday Timetable
New Year's Day is January 1.
On January 7, people celebrate the overthrow of the Khmer Rouge government.
Tet, or Lunar New Year, is celebrated in January or February. It's a significant holiday, with stores and eateries closing for several days.
April: Three days of celebrations for the Khmer New Year.
Victory Day (April 17, marking the end of the Lon Nol administration).
The anniversary of the Buddha's enlightenment falls in late April or early May.
Labor Day is May 1.
May 9 is Genocide Memorial Day, honoring those who perished under the Khmer Rouge rule.
May 11: The beginnings of joy. King's birthday is May 22.
June 8 is the Queen's birthday.

Feast of the Ancestors is in September.

The Constitution Day is September 24.

Buddhist 'Lent' (offerings to the monks) ends in October.

October 30–November 1 is Norodom Sihanouk's anniversary.

November: Festival of Water.

National Day is November 9.

Christmas is on December 25.

Vietnam and Cambodia travel guide 2023-2024

Vietnam and Cambodia travel guide 2023-2024

GASTRONOMIC PLEASURE

Vietnam eatery

Vietnam is a culinary enthusiast's dream come true. Distinguished by its use of seasonal, full-bodied tastes and vivid hues, Vietnamese food is regarded as some of the world's healthiest and tastiest. Vietnam provides an abundance of eating alternatives that are guaranteed to entice your taste buds, ranging from fine dining establishments to street food carts.

Ga Ngon is among Vietnam's top traditional dining establishments.

Ga Ngon is a distinctive restaurant in Vietnam that serves traditional cuisine in a setting that is purely Vietnamese. With a menu that features up to 180 items, it embodies the spirit of the local cuisine. The American magazine Triprow named it "The culinary place to eat once in a lifetime" after it opened in 2016. Since then, it has rapidly grown in popularity.

Ga Ngon, which is situated in the capital city of Hanoi, benefits from easy access to a wide range of premium ingredients. The food is cooked to the greatest standards, guaranteeing delicious tastes. The restaurant creates bold and flavorful dishes using a variety of seasonings like chili, pepper, dill, guise leaf, wormwood, galangal, turmeric, pepper, garlic, chili, lemongrass, and lemon leaf. Typical Vietnamese ingredients used in the restaurant's menu include chicken, glutinous rice, buffalo meat, goat meat, fish, and pure Vietnamese vegetables like onions, garlic, carrots, potatoes, and broccoli.

Ga Ngon's dedication to conserving and advancing traditional Vietnamese cuisine is what sets it apart. With an emphasis on local specialties, it provides guests with a singular chance to savor the genuine tastes of Vietnam. For those interested in learning more about Vietnamese food, the restaurant is highly recommended because of its warm and welcoming ambiance and welcoming personnel.

Location:
Ga Ngon Ha Dong branch: Yen Nghia, Ha Dong, Hanoi (near Highway 6), welcome gate to Do Nghia urban area

0967.886.202 – 0987.888.502 is the phone number.

De Nui 9 is the best restaurant in Vietnam with goat meat dishes.

For those who wish to experience the distinct flavor of goat meat in Hanoi, the De Nui 9 restaurant is a must-visit location. The restaurant serves a variety of delectable meals cooked with goat flesh, such as its well-known Goat Stew, which was named the "World's Best Food" by the American gourmet publication Food American.

The restaurant's rustic and rural décor gives guests a warm, welcoming feeling that transports them to the countryside of Vietnam. The location is made more charming by the bamboo forests, jade orchids, and wooden tables and chairs.

The Goat Stew, which combines soft goat flesh, lotus seeds, green beans, shiitake mushrooms, and a variety of spices, is one of the restaurants De Nui 9's most well-liked dishes. For those who enjoy spicy and savory food, this meal is a must.

The De Nui 9 restaurant has gained recognition and appeal, making it a popular choice for both visitors and residents. Since the restaurant might get busy, it's best to reserve a table in advance to prevent having to wait. Make sure to visit De Nui 9 restaurant for a unique dining experience if you want to enjoy real Vietnamese food.

Address: Le Trong Tan, An Khanh, Hoai Duc, Hanoi; Townhouse A18, Lot 1, Geleximco urban area
Phone: 0987.326.445 – 0963.312.445

Sen 60 Ly Thai To is among Vietnam's greatest buffet restaurants.

A posh dining destination for foodies, Sen 60 Ly Thai To Buffet Restaurant is situated in the center of Hanoi. The restaurant has three levels with a contemporary, open layout. It serves a large variety of Vietnamese and foreign cuisine. The kitchen and reception area are located on the first floor, while the delicious buffet is served to customers on the second and third floors.

With more than 200 items on the menu, the restaurant offers a variety of world cuisines from countries like Korea, Japan, France, and delicacies from all three provinces of Vietnam. Meat fans may savor meals made with goat, beef, hog, and octopuses, while seafood lovers can feast on scallops, oysters, lobsters, and octopuses.

Sen 60 Ly Thai To is the newest member of the SEN family, yet it doesn't stop foreign visitors from appreciating its opulent ambiance and lavish buffet. A white lotus, a symbol of elegance and purity, is used to compare the eatery. For those who enjoy delicious meals and a sophisticated setting, Sen 60 Ly Thai To is a must-visit location in Hanoi.

Address: Hoan Kiem District, Hanoi; No. 60 Ly Thai To Street, Trang Tien Ward

02439744192 – 02439744193.

The best restaurant in Vietnam that combines European and Asian traditions is KOTO Van Mieu.

The Temple of Literature, one of Hanoi's most well-liked tourist destinations, is not far from the KOTO Van Mieu restaurant. This KOTO flagship restaurant has served customers from all over the world and has been instrumental in promoting the company's goal of giving impoverished kids in Vietnam training in hospitality and life skills. A fantastic place to hang out with friends or coworkers is the second-floor

Temple Bar. Offering a wide array of beverages, including as KOTO's famous cocktails and smoothies, the Temple Bar offers a tranquil haven away from the bustle of Hanoi's crowded streets. There is free WiFi at the pub as well.

Situated on the third level, the Graduate Gallery serves as a function space ideal for gatherings and functions. It celebrates past KOTO trainees whose professional achievement can be attributed to their training. Present Trainees get inspiration from the Graduate Gallery, which shows them that a better future is possible. The space can hold up to 150 people for big dinner parties, cocktail parties, and other special occasions.

Scan code for major restaurants in Vietnam

With an emphasis on using products that are fresh and locally produced, KOTO Van Mieu restaurant offers a distinctive blend of Vietnamese and foreign cuisine. The popular KOTO burger, authentic Vietnamese pho, and a variety of vegetarian and gluten-free

alternatives are among the delicacies available to patrons. Not only is the cuisine at KOTO Van Mieu excellent, but it also has a significant social influence. "Know One, Teach One," or KOTO, is a humanitarian company that offers underprivileged young people in Vietnam employment and training possibilities. When patronizing KOTO Van Mieu, diners are not only indulging in a delicious meal but also helping the neighborhood and a noble cause. All things considered, KOTO Van Mieu is more than simply a restaurant; it's a destination that provides a distinctive eating experience with a significant social goal.
Address: 59 Dong Da, Hanoi's Temple of Literature
Telephone: 04-7470337

❖ Cambodian cuisine you must taste

When visiting Cambodia, tourists frequently take pleasure in Fish Amok. This is a kind of steamed curry fish that gets flavor from the steam. It is excellent but not overly hot (because, as previously indicated, Cambodian cookery tends to employ more herbs than spices, unlike neighboring Thailand and

Vietnam). The food is so soft that it frequently comes apart on a fork. The meal is frequently presented with a little coconut cream on top and served on a banana leaf.

Although Fish Amok—a Khmer adaptation of a Thai meal—is sometimes said to as Cambodia's national cuisine, its popularity among the local populace is quite low. Try it out, then. However, try a few of these meals as well:

Because both are so abundant, rice and freshwater fish play major parts in the Khmer diet. A national cuisine, amok is prepared with fish, curry paste, and coconut milk.

After combining all the ingredients, they are cooked and placed in banana leaf cups with coconut cream on top. Amok chouk, or snails with curry cooked within their shells, is another popular kind. The ideal accompaniment to it is a serving of steaming hot rice.

- ➢ Samlor Karkoo is a blended vegetable and green fruit soup made with papaya, jackfruit, and bananas.

- ➢ Samlor Machou Yuon is a tart "Vietnamese" soup made with tamarind and fresh fish.

Many Cambodian homes enjoy making samlor machu trey soup because it tastes good and is very simple to prepare. Fish, garlic, lemongrass, celery, tamarind juice, bean sprouts, pineapple, and seasoning with salt, sugar, and fish sauce are among its components.

Before serving, a lot of people like to sprinkle some spicy chili pepper and fresh green herbs on top.

- ➢ Bok Svay: Dried fish or prawns are typically served with a pounded green mango salad.
- ➢ A pepper sauce called Tuk Meric is used to dip grilled meat. It is composed of lime juice, salt, and ground Kampot pepper.
- ➢ Num Banchok is a Cambodian curry served with cold rice noodles.

❖ Cambodia's top restaurants to visit

1. The Restaurant's Friends

Renowned for its innovative interpretations of both traditional Asian and Western cuisines, this restaurant is among the best in all of Cambodia. Both the colorful yet laid-back décor and the plating are exquisite here. This restaurant is ideal for hosting a

large, elegant gathering of loved ones. Critics sometimes write incredibly positive things about the meal. Additionally, Friends the Restaurant in Phnom Penh, Cambodia has been assisting marginalized kids and street children since 2007 by collaborating with Friends International.
Address: 215-215 Street 13, Phnom Penh
Two-person price: INR 2000

2. As Dakshin's
Renowned for its Indian cuisine, this restaurant is among the best in all of Cambodia. Both North and South Indian food are served here; their butter chicken and garlic naan are particularly well-liked. It's the ideal spot to chill out with friends after a hectic day because of the laid-back decor. Here, you may also sample Asian or Singaporean cuisine. The Indian population in Siem Reap, Cambodia, is not fond of most Indian eateries, but Dakshin's is a favorite among all of them.
Location: Siem Reap's Old Market
Two-person price: INR 1800

3. Mood Café

This lively eatery is a good vegetarian alternative for those watching what they eat. They provide amazing vegan food; their nomad burgers and zucchini noodles are a must-try. The freshly squeezed juices are served here, and the inventive use of vegetable colors to create magical plating will do wonders for your hunger. This restaurant is undoubtedly at the top of the list of vegetarian eateries in Siem Reap, Cambodia, and you really shouldn't miss it.
Location: Siem Reap, 715 Hup Guan Street
Two-person price: INR 1500

4. II Salamander

Without a doubt, one of the best restaurants in Cambodia is this wonderful establishment. The restaurant, which doubles as a pizzeria and deli, is quite popular. You will probably discover the best Italian in this nation with them. No Cambodia tour guide would ever tell you about their excellent pizzas, which are as good as anything you get in Italy, according to the few Westerners who visit this cafe. They also serve other classic Italian foods including lasagna, carbonara, and cold cut platters.
Location: Khan Mittapheap, Sihanoukville; N 371, Ekareach Blvd.

Two-person price: INR 2000

5. Restaurant Langka

This little, eccentric, packed French bistro in the heart of Phnom Penh radiates a type of French flair that is uncommon among Cambodian eateries. Many people like the variety of wines, duck, and meat that are served here. If you don't make reservations in advance, be prepared to wait in line for a while!
51 Pasteur Street, Phnom Penh
Two-person price: INR 1500

6.Ten. Haschi

Hachi is a great spot to take a date if you're looking for a great place to have Japanese food. The food is excellent, and the decor is elegant. At Hachi, you can hassle-free savor some of the greatest sushi available in the nation. The cuisine tastes even better because of the flavorful, fresh ingredients. The experience is further enhanced by the prompt and kind service provided by the workers.
Location: Phnom Penh, 26 Sothearos Boulevard
Two-person price: INR 4,000

7. Malis Phnom Penh Restaurant

Malis Restaurant offers modern cuisine in a traditional Khmer setting. Celebrity chef Luu Meng of Cambodia set out to discover and bring back the country's distinctive flavors, and he is doing a great job of it at the Malis restaurant.

Malis Restaurant offers an exciting assortment of Cambodian specialties that you have never seen before. They combine traditional cooking methods with unique twists on ingredients and textures. Malis Restaurant offers a selection of unique vintage wines in addition to its menu.

Address: 136 Norodom Boulevard, Cambodia, Phnom Penh

Hours of Operation: 6:30 AM to 10 PM

Bookings: The Official Website

Phone: (0)15 814 888, +855

Vietnam and Cambodia travel guide 2023-2024

Scan for major restaurants in Cambodia

VISA AND ENTRY REQUIREMENTS AND ACCOMMODATION OPTIONS

What Are Vietnam's Visa Requirements?

Most international travelers to Vietnam are required to obtain a valid visa, under the country's travel regulations. Applying online for an e-Visa is the quickest and most straightforward method to obtain one.

In order to satisfy the Vietnam visa requirements for 2023-2024, you will need to fulfill specific requirements and submit an online application with a few simple papers.

Additionally, you have to be a citizen of one of the nations that accept e-Visas.

requirements for getting an electronic visa for Vietnam

You have to be visiting Vietnam for one of the following reasons and for a maximum of ninety days:

Journeys

Company

Go see friends or family

Invest in businesses in Vietnam
Work or temporary work
Reporting
Examines
official meeting or excursion
To extend your stay in Vietnam, you can apply for a new visa before your current one expires and enter the country with an eVisa. But, in order to apply to the Vietnam Immigration Department on your behalf, you need to be sponsored by a Vietnamese agency, organization, or person.
Documents needed to apply for a visa to Vietnam
You must satisfy the following conditions for a Vietnamese electronic visa in order to receive the online visa:
passport from a nation that qualifies
a digital scan of the passport's biographical page
digital image for passport
Card, debit or credit
Email address

What is the visa exemption for Vietnam?
Certain nationals are excluded from needing a visa for brief travels. This implies that they are allowed entry and a limited number of days of stay within the

nation without a visa. Depending on the visitor's nationality, there are different time limits.

Travelers without a visa just need a current passport from a nation where Vietnam does not require one.

For lengthier visits, though, even citizens of these nations will require a visa. Living, studying, working, or engaging in any other activity in Vietnam that isn't covered by the conditions of visa exemption will also require a visa.

Additional Guidelines and Conditions for Vietnam eVisa

It's crucial to confirm that your passport satisfies the following requirements before using the e-Visa to enter Vietnam:

valid for a minimum of half a year following arrival in Vietnam

two or more pages without stamps

The e-Visa permits repeated entries into Vietnam throughout its ninety-day validity period.

For the length of their visit, visitors are required to have a copy of their eVisa with them.

Do kids need an eVisa to enter Vietnam?

Children who are included on their parent's passport and who are 14 years of age or less may also be listed on their parent's e-Visa application.

An additional visa application has to be submitted for:

children with their own passports

Any young person older than 14

Fees and Application for a Visa

Because you'll be filling out an online application, the actual procedure of applying is nearly the same as applying for an e-visa. There are a few notable variations, though, particularly in terms of the costs.

You will need to send a digital photo or scan of your passport along with a digital passport-style photo of yourself, just like you would for an e-visa.

You will have the option of a 30-day or 90-day visa, with the latter costing a little bit extra.

In order to use the company's service, you must pay them a charge when you apply. This amount varies, but it is often $20 or less.

Like the e-visa, the actual visa charge is $25, which you will need to pay at the immigration counter in U.S. dollars when you arrive in Vietnam (this is also referred to as a "stamping fee" by many of these firms).

After submitting your application, you should get your "invitation letter" over email in a matter of hours to days. You will need to wait in immigration once you get to the airport in order to exchange your invitation letter for the real visa.

Travelers will be called out individually by immigration officers, thus the length of the wait will depend on both the volume of passengers and the speed at which your name is called.

❖ Cambodian Accommodation Options.

Accommodations for Families in Siem Reap

I think Siem Reap has partially stolen my heart. The city itself is fantastic, yet it seems very gritty at times. People speed through the streets on scooters, motorcycles, and Tuk Tuks, leaving a dusty afterglow. There is food everywhere you turn. You are surrounded by restaurants that invite you inside. For millennia, Angkor Wat has waited for your arrival in a serene location just outside of the city.

You are in the center of Cambodia, right in the thick of everything!

It goes without saying that one of our top priorities upon arriving in Cambodia was to view the Angkor Wat Temples. I searched for the greatest spot to stay in Siem Reap with kids since I wanted to be close to well-known temples. I've located one!

Top Hotels in Siem Reap for Families

We had an easy decision. Dreams of Navutu Resort and Spa! Nothing compared to this location, which perfectly met our requirements. Lovely property with rooms sets apart for the kids and us. Cozy mattresses, the biggest bathtub and shower, and friendly room service. Here, we were content to laze about the three pools while enjoying virgin drinks and watching Katie-Lee and Lily play in the water in front of us. A tranquil haven and the greatest hotel in Siem Reap! What this hotel has that the kids will adore:

the option to select from three distinct kinds of pools! The activities kids may play in the really beautiful, verdant garden paths

The wonderful personnel, who genuinely adore children and go above and above to make them happy Cambodia's Krong Siem Reap

Rating of four stars

Vietnam and Cambodia travel guide 2023-2024

Rates for rooms: Couples rooms start at $70 US per night, which includes breakfast buffet.
Families, couples, and singles all stay here.

Scan code for Cambodia Accomodation options
Phnom Penh for Families
Penang, Ph. Cambodia, the Capital of the Kingdom of Wonders! The jungle of concrete, its past seeping through its pores. You've come to the correct spot if you're looking to learn more about the nation and its recent history. The king's residence and several museums may be found here. You will become lost in this area amidst the millions of speeding

motorbikes and automobiles that are always swerving into and out of traffic. The magnificent Mekong River and the center of a formerly bustling port may be found here.

It makes sense to choose a location that is close to the city center and the river while searching for reasonably priced lodging in Phnom Penh with children. In this manner, you won't have to pay a lot of money for transportation to and from the main drag's eateries and excitement. You will spend a lot of time weaving through the streets during rush hour if your Phnom Penh lodging is distant from the city center.

An inexpensive hotel in Phnom Penh

The Tea House Asian Urban Resort is where we have decided to stay. As the pricing indicates, we chose to stay at a budget hotel in Phnom Penh rather than spend a few dollars in the capital. There was something lacking even though the setting was cozy, the restaurant's cuisine was excellent, and the service was excellent. This hotel is located in the heart of the high-rise metropolis, yet it's only a short Tuk Tuk ride from the river. As one might anticipate from a budget motel, the lone window in the room was facing another wall. Nevertheless, the accommodation had all we needed for the stay and was immaculate with a contemporary style. If you're looking for a reasonably priced place to stay, I'd describe it as a budget boutique hotel and would suggest a stay here. Images from hotelscombined.com of Tea House Asian Urban Resort

Address: 242 Street, Phnom Penh, Cambodia 12200
A rating of three stars
Room Prices: $32 USD per night
Families, couples, and singles all stay here.

Family-Friendly Kep Residence
Kep exceeded my expectations. This location absolutely begs for leisure and indulging in the regional food. Chairs and hammocks dotted the length of Kep beach. Little groups of people relaxing with a variety of foods and beverages could be seen for as far as the eye could see. Everyone was grinning, whether they were visitors or not, families, couples, or both.
Fresh crabs taken right from the ocean and placed in open kitchens fill the bustling crab markets. My mouth is watering, the ambiance is captivating, and the fragrance is fantastic!

Where should families stay in Kep? There are several options. You are only a short Tuk Tuk ride from the crab markets or the Kep beach, depending on where you stay. Allow me to assist you in selecting your Kep lodging.

Kep Hotel: Ideal for Families
I chose Raingsey Bungalow Kep for our stay. Situated within a short stroll from Kep National Park and the well-known Crab Market. Our family was well-suited to the house we owned. Nice mattresses and separate rooms for the kids and us. air conditioning, all for a really low cost. It's always pleasant to lounge by the pool and watch our kids play. Nothing was greater or different here. The breakfast buffet located on the upper level of the reception was excellent. Excellent cuisine, lovely scenery, kind and accommodating staff—Raingsey Bungalow Kep has it all!

Place: Thmey Village, Prey Thom Commune, Kep, Cambodia, Kep 07503, Cambodia Crab Market
Room costs: $54 per night
Families, couples, and singles all stay here.

Vietnam and Cambodia travel guide 2023-2024

❖ Vietnam Accommodation Options

1. Six Feelings with Dao

Con Dao, a group of sixteen islands in Vietnam with sweeping vistas of the South China Sea, is an unrivaled natural treasure. These isolated islands are thought to offer the greatest scuba diving and snorkeling in all of Vietnam. They are turtle breeding grounds, home to immaculate coral reefs, and teeming with an amazing diversity of marine life.

The luxurious resort Six Senses Con Dao is a suitable location for a decadent yet ecologically conscious family holiday, where visitors can enjoy the unspoiled beauty of the surrounding environment with the green turtles who call Con Dao home. The resort, which is well-known for its strong dedication to sustainability, works to reduce its environmental impact and carbon footprint in both its lodging and spa.

Airy, high-ceilinged contemporary villas stand-alone amid lush foliage, offering breathtaking views from their individual infinity pools that face the ocean. This opulent beach resort in Vietnam offers an abundance of tempting aquatic activities, spa services, and dining options for both adults and kids.

Reasons your family should think about staying at this resort: Six Senses Con Dao has a whole program specifically for its younger guests. Kids may choose between culinary and sustainability workshops at the kids' club, feed the chickens in the organic gardens, take part in environmental activities, and learn about turtle protection. Additionally, this opulent family resort provides a variety of adventure and health activities for the parents, like singing bowl therapy, yoga, diving, and boating. Most importantly, the resort is "totally walled off to the outer world...guarantees complete solitude and seclusion—knowing your family is cocooned in nature," says Hannah Loughlin, director of sales and marketing at Six Senses Con Dao.

Family rooms: The Deluxe Ocean Front Villa is perfect for a small family; the Family Villa, a two-level duplex, accommodates a larger family; and the three- and four-bedroom Ocean Residences, standalone villas with shared infinity pool and spacious living and dining areas, are perfect for those exciting family reunions—especially valuable in the post-pandemic era. Six Senses Con Dao offers families three types of oceanfront luxury accommodation along the Vietnam coast.

2. The InterContinental Long Beach Resort in Phu Quoc

The stunning island of Phu Quoc is situated just under neighboring Cambodia, off the southwest coast of Vietnam. Here, the landscape changes from white sand beaches fringed with palm trees to mountains and deep tropical woods. Rich evergreen woods cover more than half of the island, which is a National Park. Diverse marine life and healthy coral reefs may be found in the seas around the park.

The InterContinental Phu Quoc Long Beach Resort is located in this little piece of heaven. It is the perfect luxury family hotel location in Vietnam, nestled in total seclusion on one of the island's most sought-after locations, Long Beach, and only 20 minutes from the quaint town of Duong Dong.

Families with adventurous palates will enjoy all six of the InterContinental Phu Quoc Long Beach Resort's culinary options, which range from native Vietnamese specialties at Sora & Umi to comfortable Italian favorites at Ombra and grilled meals at Sea Shack. Adults may enjoy cocktail mixing while admiring the stunning sunset views at INK 360, the island's tallest sky bar.

Why your family should stay at this resort: The 250 square meter Planet Trekkers children's club, located in the opulent accommodations, offers a wide range of entertaining, culturally themed, and completely supervised indoor and outdoor activities. When it's time to cool off, dive into The Splash, one of the resort's four swimming pools! With water slides and inflatable toys for the smaller ones, the pool is a family favorite. And at the HARNN Heritage Spa, which has won several awards, indulge in regionally inspired wellness treatments to feel refreshed after a day of family activity.
Family accommodations: The InterContinental Phu Quoc Long Beach Resort's Family Suites are designed with kids in mind. Games and books abound in the room's tent, and the suites have kid-sized bathrobes and slippers.

3.Hoi An's Anantara Resort
Anantara Hoi An Resort, located in Vietnam, combines history, tradition, and the splendor of nature. Your family may stay in opulence while yet being able to stroll to one of the country's most well-known historic districts.

Families with a particular interest in history and architecture will enjoy Hoi An old town's blend of architectural styles and eras, which includes the famous Japanese Covered Bridge, colorful French colonial buildings, and elaborate Vietnamese tube houses, all illuminated by lanterns.

A visit to the My Son ruins, if you can drag yourself away from the UNESCO-designated Hoi An, is highly recommended. Here, visitors may take in the handcrafted goods offered by local artist communities, contemporary art galleries, teahouses, ancient shrines, and the peaceful Ang Bang Beach.

With its lush gardens and breathtaking sunset views, the Anantara Hoi An Resort, which fronts the Thu Bon River, has a backdrop fit for a picture. Families may enjoy riverfront dining with options ranging from fresh Vietnamese cuisines to contemporary bistro-style food, take a sunset river cruise, and indulge in spa treatments that will leave them feeling blissfully relaxed.

Why your family should book a stay at the Anantara Hoi An Resort: According to Kate Jones, the area director of public relations, visitors can "dive into local experiences, including Vietnamese cooking classes, traditional Non La hat and lantern painting opportunities, and visiting local villages for a slice of Vietnamese life." Younger visitors may enjoy educational activities at the Kids' Club, and if they'd like to take a day excursion throughout the area, families can pick from a variety of options.

Family accommodations: The resort has 13 pairs of interconnecting rooms for families that prefer seclusion yet near proximity (additional cribs, beds, and bunk beds can be requested).

Scan code for Vietnam accommodation options

Domestic transportation in Vietnam

Vietnam's railways

Traveling across Vietnam by rail can be both instructive and peaceful, with an average speed of 40 km/h. Vietnam Railways is in charge of overseeing a single 2,600km network of tracks that connects the North and South. From Ho Chi Minh City to the Chinese border, the railroad meanders throughout the nation. For a little more comfort, go for the four-berth cabins and soft chairs, or treat yourself to one of the exclusive tourists sleeping cars that are now available on numerous important lines. Because many of the current rails are from colonial times, the train line is undergoing restoration, so do your homework before you visit.

Address of the Hanoi Train Station: 120 Lê Duẩn, Cửa Nam, Hoàn Kiếm, Hà Nội and Vietnam
The train station for Ho Chi Minh City is located at 1 Nguyễn Thông, Phường 9, Quận 3, Hồ Chí Minh, Vietnam.

Purchasing rail passes in Vietnam

Depending on the route, you may purchase your train tickets from counters at Vietnam's train stations days or months in advance of your journey. Additionally, a number of travel businesses as well as Vietnam's official railway booking website sell train tickets online.

Children who are older than five must pay the full price of the ticket.

Every carriage on every train has a western-style, squat toilet on both ends.

Reunification Express Trains offer freight forwarding and luggage transportation services.

The Express of Reunification

In reality, the Reunification Express isn't a train. Completed by the French in 1936, the route links Hanoi and Ho Chi Minh City. The gorgeous voyage lasts for 36 hours and stops in Phan Thiet, Danang, Nha Trang, and Hue. Five Reunification Express trips depart from Hanoi and Ho Chi Minh City every day at 7:30 PM, 10 PM, 6 AM, 9 AM, and 1:10 PM, offering a leisurely yet unforgettable travel. Hard seat, soft seat, hard sleeper, and soft sleeper are the four classes available. There are four sleepers in each of the cabins, and the bedding is basic.

Vietnam and Cambodia travel guide 2023-2024

In Vietnam, bus

Budget tourists are finding more and more usage of open-tour buses, particularly in the middle and southern parts of Vietnam. Buses between popular locations including Hanoi, Hue, Hoi An, Nha Trang, Da Lat, Mui Ne, and Ho Chi Minh City run on a regular and dependable schedule. The majority of open tour buses have deeply reclining seats or are sleeper buses. You can find the most reputable open-tour bus companies with a quick Google search. Unless you're traveling during a Vietnamese holiday, in which case you should reserve tickets at least two weeks in advance, we advise booking one or two days in advance.

Bicycles in Vietnam

Motorbikes are the most practical means of transportation for short trips and are considered the embodiment of Vietnamese culture. If you're an independent traveler, you might like the excitement and breathtaking scenery of long-distance motorcycling. On Vietnam's streets, inexperienced drivers should exercise caution and pay attention to the local driving style, which emphasizes ebb and flow over strict adherence to the law. Nearly every city has motorbike rental stores. Scooters and mopeds range in price from 150,000 to 300,000 VND a day, depending on the quality of the bike. If you are renting for a period longer than a week, you may be required to leave a deposit or your passport. Never leave your motorcycle alone in Vietnam. Wear a helmet at all times. If your motorcycle is left in a parking lot, make sure to verify the ticket number.

Vietnam bicycle tourism

Vietnam will make you fall in love with riding a bicycle again, whether you're a serious rider or just want to do short rides sometimes. While cycling is accessible in the metropolis, Vietnam's coastal resorts and rural villages are ideal for trips on two wheels. In actuality, bicycle excursions are among the top guided tours in the nation. These may be found throughout Central Vietnam and the Mekong Delta. Bicycle rentals in locations like Hoi An and Hue can take you practically everywhere you wish to go (many locals do so). Rentals typically cost between 20,000 and 30,000 VND per day, or around $1.

Within Cambodia, transportation

By bus: The most popular and reasonably priced mode of transportation in Cambodia. Numerous bus companies operate throughout the nation, providing a range of services from budget to first-class. Families should select a trustworthy business with an excellent safety record. Mekong Express, Virak Buntham Express, and Giant Ibis are a few well-known bus operators.

Here are some instances of bus prices in Cambodia between well-known locations:
$10–$15 from Phnom Penh to Siem Reap
$5–$10 from Phnom Penh to Battambang
$5–$10 from Siem Reap to Battambang
Sihanoukville to Phnom Penh: $9–$15
Sihanoukville to Siem Reap: $12–$17

You might want to think about renting a private vehicle or van if you are traveling with a large family or have a lot of luggage. Although it costs more than the bus, this is more convenient and pleasant. You have two options: use a reliable travel agency to reserve a car, or haggle directly with the driver over the price.

Although they are more expensive than buses and tuk-tuks, taxis are also accessible in Cambodia's major cities and towns. While tuk-tuks are an enjoyable and cost-effective mode of transportation for short excursions, extended trips are not advised.

❖ Tips for Health and Safety

Health advice
Obtain a vaccine. Consult your physician about the required vaccines for your trip, considering your age, general health, and itinerary. Travel to Vietnam and Cambodia is sometimes advised to get certain immunizations, such as typhoid, diphtheria, tetanus, and hepatitis A and B.
Cappucinate water. In much of Vietnam and Cambodia, tap water is unsafe to drink, therefore stay away from it. Bottled water is affordable and readily accessible.
Watch what you put in your mouth. In Vietnam and Cambodia, street food is a fun and tasty meal option, but you should be selective about what you choose. Steer clear of food that has been left out for an extended period of time or that has not been

cooked completely. Additionally, unless you are certain that the fruits and vegetables have been completely cleaned, it is advisable to avoid eating them raw.

Apply bug repellant. In Vietnam and Cambodia, mosquitoes are prevalent and may transmit illnesses including dengue fever and malaria. When you're outside, apply insect repellent with at least 20% DEET to any exposed skin.

Apply sunscreen. Vietnam and Cambodia have extremely intense sun, therefore even on overcast days, all exposed skin should use sunscreen with an SPF of 30 or greater.

Safety advice

Pay attention to your surroundings. Avoid wandering alone at night and keep your belongings near to you as preventative measures against small-time theft.

When crossing the street, use caution. Cambodian and Vietnamese traffic may be extremely hectic. When crossing the street, make careful to check both ways, and even then, be ready for unexpected automobile traffic.

Respect regional traditions. Given that both Vietnam and Cambodia are Buddhist nations, it's critical to respect regional traditions and customs. For instance, when you visit temples and other places of worship, dress modestly.

Make a fallback plan. Have a backup plan in place in case of an emergency, such as a misplaced passport or illness. This might be having a copy of your insurance card and passport with you, or it could be having the number of a friend or relative who can assist you in touch.

SHOPPING IN VIETNAM AND CAMBODIA

Purchasing in Hanoi

Silk, handicrafts, rice paper goods, trinkets, bandanas, and vibrant Ao Dais make Hanoi an ideal destination for shoppers! Here, we'll give you a tour of the top shopping destinations in Hanoi as well as what to buy while in Vietnam.

1. *Market Street Nightlife*

With almost 4,000 stores beneath the starry sky, the Street Night Market is a lively and exciting place to browse for Vietnamese goods! For a little portion of what it would cost elsewhere, you may get a wide variety of apparel, shoes, fashion accessories, home appliances, arts and crafts including water puppet sculptures, and souvenirs. The Night Market is the best place to go for affordable shopping in Vietnam and has an enormous selection of street food options, including bun thang, La Vong grilled fish, pho, banh mi, and bun cha.

Location: Old Quarter
Hours: 6:00 p.m. to 11:00 p.m.
Friday, Saturday, and Sunday are the open days.

2. Flower Market in Quang Ba

A visual and emotional delight, this marketplace is filled with bright daisy, cherry, rose, orchid, and sunflower blooms. Walking through this market and inhaling its aromas is an experience you will never forget. You would not want to overlook taking a photo of this gorgeous setting! Without picking up a few fresh flowers here, your shopping in Vietnam Hanoi is only halfway complete.
Location: Tay Ho's Au Co Street
Hours: 2:00 am to 12:00 pm

3. Xuan Dong Market
Everything from seafood, meat, and vegetables to T-shirts, purses, fashion accessories, Vietnamese conical hats, and handicrafts are sold at wholesale prices in this two-story indoor market. The

welcoming store owners provide an insight into Vietnamese society.
Location: Hoan Kiem's Dong Xuan Street
Hours: 06:00 am–07:00 pm

4. Pottery Village of Bat Trang
Everything made of pottery, including upscale dinnerware, religious objects, and trinkets, is sold in this ceramic hamlet. Additionally, you may work with a potter to create your own unique artwork by turning the clay on the ceramic table. This is the ideal location to get top-notch Vietnamese souvenirs to give to loved ones or to make your vacation unforgettable.
Location: Gia Lam's Bat Trang Village

Shopping at Cambodia's unique market

Southeast Asia's "land of villages," Cambodia, is well-known for its growing tourist industry. The popularity of the local flea markets has increased as a result of the nation's burgeoning tourism industry. Their exquisitely carved, handcrafted mementos capture the eye. Numerous locally made goods, including silks, pottery, jewelry, spices, and much more, may be found in Cambodia.

What Should I Buy in Vietnam?

1. Artworks

Due to its historical Khmer architecture and Buddhist influence, travelers may find a wide variety of handicrafts in Cambodia, including painted Buddha statues, Angkorian sculptures, carved clay pots, and more.

Where to buy: Siem Reap's flea markets, including as the Siem Reap Art Center Market and AHA Fair Trade Village.

2. Wine Made from Rice

Homemade liquor known locally as "Sra" or rice wine is quite popular. This highly sought-after rice wine is frequently flavored with fruits, spices, and therapeutic herbs in hand-painted bottles.

Where to buy: Siem Reap's local marketplaces and the Aeon mall in Phnom Penh.

3. Fabrics

The marketplaces in Cambodia provide handmade silk and cotton textiles that are locally created and colored. The natural plant fibers used to create the soft, vividly colored textiles are used to make a variety of goods, including scarves, purses, and garments. Famous Cambodian textiles include the Khmer Golden Silk and the traditional Krama cotton scarf.

Where to buy: Siem Reap's Made in Cambodia Market and Samatoa shop.

Malls for shopping in Cambodia

1. Phnom Penh's Aeon Mall

One of the biggest and nicest malls in Cambodia is Aeon Mall, which is located in the nation's capital, Phnom Penh. Huge supermarkets and worldwide brand stores like Starbucks, Mango, Gucci, and so on are owned by this mall. There are two locations of this well-known mall in Phnom Penh.

What to buy: Shopaholics may indulge in opulent apparel and cosmetics lines as well as nutritious edibles like chia seeds, himalayan pink salt, and organic coconut oil.

Hours: 9:00 AM–10:30 PM

2. Penang's Central Market

Built in 1937 in Phnom Penh, the Central Market is known as Phsar Thmei. One of the main draws here is the dome-shaped building, which is well worth

seeing. Although a bit pricey, the market is full with stores and food vendors selling traditional Cambodian fare. This store also features a sizable area that sells fresh meat, rice, and other seasonings. Things to purchase include postcards, spices, delectable trinkets, gold jewelry, traditional Cambodian attire, and inexpensive electronics.
Hours: 7 A.M. to 6 P.M.

Scan for shopping markets in vietnam and cambodia

CONCLUSION

❖ Packing Necessities

The following is a list of necessities to bring for family trips to Vietnam and Cambodia:

Clothing
Airy, light, and loose-fitting apparel
To defend against the sun and insects, wear long sleeves and pants.
a sun hat and shades
A cover-up and bathing suit
cozy footwear for touring and strolling
A raincoat or rain jacket
Personal hygiene
Sunscreen having at least a 30 SPF rating
insect repellent that contains 20% or more DEET
Glycerin for hands
toothpaste and a toothbrush

Vietnam and Cambodia travel guide 2023-2024

both conditioner and shampoo
Bars
saline wipes and bandages
Pain killers
OTC allergy drugs
Any prescription drugs you require
Other necessities
passport and, if necessary, visa
Currency (credit cards and cash)
Insurance for travel
Phone and camera charger
An electrical outlet adapter, if necessary
Word book First-aid package
Children's beverages and snacks
For young people
Wipes and diapers (if necessary)
Breast milk or formula (if needed)
Swap out your clothing
favorite games or pastimes
Insect repellant and sunscreen suitable for children

Language in Vietnam

Vietnamese is the official language of Vietnam and is spoken by over 95% of the population. It is a tonal language, meaning that the meaning of a word can changes depending on the tone used. There are six tones in Vietnamese, which can be difficult for foreigners to master.
However, there are a few basic Vietnamese phrases that can be useful for family travelers, such as:
Xin chào (Sin chao) - Hello
Cảm ơn (Kahm uhn) - Thank you
Xin lỗi (Sin loy) - Sorry
Tạm biệt (Tam byeet) - Goodbye
Có bao nhiêu? (Koh bao nhieu?) - How much?
Tôi muốn mua... (Toi muon mua...) - I want to buy...
Tôi không hiểu (Toi khong hieu) - I don't understand
Xin giúp tôi (Sin giup toi) - Please help me
It is also a good idea to learn a few basic Vietnamese phrases for food and drink, such as:
Tôi đói (Toi doi) - I'm hungry
Tôi khát (Toi khat) - I'm thirsty
Tôi muốn ăn... (Toi muon an...) - I want to eat...
Tôi muốn uống... (Toi muon uong...) - I want to drink...
Ngon quá! (Ngon qua!) - Delicious!

While it is not necessary to speak Vietnamese fluently to travel in Vietnam, learning a few basic phrases can help you to get around more easily and communicate with locals. It is also a great way to show respect for Vietnamese culture.

Language in Cambodia

The official language of Cambodia is Khmer, which is spoken by nearly 90% of the population. English is also widely spoken, especially among younger Cambodians and those in the tourism industry.
Here are some basic Khmer phrases that can be useful for family travelers:
Hello: Chum reap suor
Goodbye: Lea hai
Thank you: Orkun
You're welcome: Sok san
Please: Choum
Excuse me: Chot te
Yes: Choe
No: Ott
Do you speak English?: Ning pteas eng leah?
Here are some additional phrases that may be helpful when traveling with children:
Child: Dek

Baby: Lok
Bathroom: Chhnang
Food: Aharn
Water: Neir
Milk: Nom
Sick: Chheuteal
Doctor: Lok kru
Help!: Choy!

It is also helpful to learn a few basic counting numbers in Khmer:

One: Muoy
Two: Pi
Three: Bei
Four: Buon
Five: Pram

When interacting with Cambodians, it is important to be respectful of their culture and customs. For example, it is considered rude to point at people or to speak loudly in public. It is also important to dress modestly, especially when visiting temples and other religious sites.

Dear Readers,

I hope you've enjoyed exploring the world through the pages of my travel guidebook. Your feedback is invaluable to me as an author, and I would greatly appreciate your thoughts and comments on your experience with the guide. Whether it's suggestions for improvement, highlights you particularly enjoyed, or any additional information you'd like to see in future editions, your input will help make this guide even better for fellow travelers.

Please take a moment to share your feedback with me. Your insights will contribute to creating more enriching and enjoyable travel experiences for all.

Thank you for your time, and happy travels!

Warm regards,

Ortega W. Susan

Printed in Great Britain
by Amazon